Learn Urdu with Beginner Stories

HypLern Interlinear Project
www.hyplern.com

First edition: 2025, September

Author: Unknown
Translation: Kees van den End
Foreword: Camilo Andrés Bonilla Carvajal PhD

ISBN: 978-1-989643-25-9

kees@hyplern.com
www.hyplern.com

Learn Urdu with Beginner Stories

Interlinear Urdu to English

Author
Unknown

Translation
Kees van den End

HypLern Interlinear Project
www.hyplern.com

The HypLern Method

Learning a foreign language should not mean leafing through page after page in a bilingual dictionary until one's fingertips begin to hurt. Quite the contrary, through everyday language use, friendly reading, and direct exposure to the language we can get well on our way towards mastery of the vocabulary and grammar needed to read native texts. In this manner, learners can be successful in the foreign language without too much study of grammar paradigms or rules. Indeed, Seneca expresses in his sixth epistle that "Longum iter est per praecepta, breve et efficax per exempla[1]."

The HypLern series constitutes an effort to provide a highly effective tool for experiential foreign language learning. Those who are genuinely interested in utilizing original literary works to learn a foreign language do not have to use conventional graded texts or adapted versions for novice readers. The former only distort the actual essence of literary works, while the latter are highly reduced in vocabulary and relevant content. This collection aims to bring the lively experience of reading stories as directly told by their very authors to foreign language learners.

Most excited adult language learners will at some point seek their teachers' guidance on the process of learning to read in the foreign language rather than seeking out external opinions. However, both teachers and learners lack a general reading technique or strategy. Oftentimes, students undertake the reading task equipped with nothing more than a bilingual dictionary, a grammar book, and lots of courage. These efforts often end in frustration as the student builds mis-constructed nonsensical sentences after many hours spent on an aimless translation drill.

Consequently, we have decided to develop this series of interlinear translations intended to afford a comprehensive edition of unabridged texts. These texts are presented as they were originally written with no changes in word choice or order. As a result, we have a translated piece conveying the true meaning under every word from the original work. Our readers receive then two books in just one volume: the original version and its translation.

The reading task is no longer a laborious exercise of patiently decoding unclear and seemingly complex paragraphs. What's more, reading becomes an enjoyable and meaningful process of cultural, philosophical and linguistic learning. Independent learners can then acquire expressions and vocabulary while understanding pragmatic and socio-cultural dimensions of the target language by reading in it rather than reading about it.

Our proposal, however, does not claim to be a novelty. Interlinear translation is as old as the Spanish tongue, e.g. "glosses of [Saint] Emilianus", interlinear bibles in Old German, and of course James Hamilton's work in the 1800s. About the latter, we remind the readers, that as a revolutionary freethinker he promoted the publication of Greco-Roman classic works and further pieces in diverse languages. His effort, such as ours, sought to lighten the exhausting task of looking words up in large glossaries as an educational practice: "if there is any thing which fills reflecting men with melancholy and regret, it is the waste of mortal time, parental money, and puerile happiness, in the present method of pursuing Latin and Greek[2]".

Additionally, another influential figure in the same line of thought as Hamilton was John Locke. Locke was also the philosopher and translator of the Fabulae AEsopi in an interlinear plan. In 1600, he was already suggesting that interlinear texts, everyday communication, and use of the target language could be the most appropriate ways to achieve language learning:

> ...the true and genuine Way, and that which I would propose, not only as the easiest and best, wherein a Child might, without pains or Chiding, get a Language which others are wont to be whipt for at School six or seven Years together...[3]

---

1 "The journey is long through precepts, but brief and effective through examples". Seneca, Lucius Annaeus. (1961) Ad Lucilium Epistulae Morales, vol. I. London: W. Heinemann.

2 In: Hamilton, James (1829?) History, principles, practice and results of the Hamiltonian system, with answers to the Edinburgh and Westminster reviews; A lecture delivered at Liverpool; and instructions for the use of the books published on the system. Londres: W. Aylott and Co., 8, Pater Noster Row. p. 29.

3 In: Locke, John. (1693) Some thoughts concerning education. Londres: A. and J. Churchill. pp. 196-7.

Who can benefit from this edition?

We identify three kinds of readers, namely, those who take this work as a search tool, those who want to learn a language by reading authentic materials, and those attempting to read writers in their original language. The HypLern collection constitutes a very effective instrument for all of them.

1. For the first target audience, this edition represents a search tool to connect their mother tongue with that of the writer's. Therefore, they have the opportunity to read over an original literary work in an enriching and certain manner.
2. For the second group, reading every word or idiomatic expression in its actual context of use will yield a strong association between the form, the collocation, and the context. This will have a direct impact on long term learning of passive vocabulary, gradually building genuine reading ability in the original language. This book is an ideal companion not only to independent learners but also to those who take lessons with a teacher. At the same time, the continuous feeling of achievement produced during the process of reading original authors both stimulates and empowers the learner to study[1].
3. Finally, the third kind of reader will notice the same benefits as the previous ones. The proximity of a word and its translation in our interlinear texts is a step further from other collections, such as the Loeb Classical Library. Although their works might be considered the most famous in this genre, the presentation of texts on opposite pages hinders the immediate link between words and their semantic equivalence in our native tongue (or one we have a strong mastery of).

---

1 Some further ways of using the present work include:

1. As you progress through the stories, focus less on the lower line (the English translation). Instead, try to read through the upper line, staying in the foreign language as long as possible.
2. Even if you find glosses or explanatory footnotes about the mechanics of the language, you should make your own hypotheses on word formation and syntactical functions in a sentence. Feel confident about inferring your own language rules and test them progressively. You can also take notes concerning those idiomatic expressions or special language usage that calls your attention for later study.
3. As soon as you finish each text, check the reading in the original version (with no interlinear or parallel translation). This will fulfil the main goal of this

collection: bridging the gap between readers and original literary works, training them to read directly and independently.

Why interlinear?

Conventionally speaking, tiresome reading in tricky and exhausting circumstances has been the common definition of learning by texts. This collection offers a friendly reading format where the language is not a stumbling block anymore. Contrastively, our collection presents a language as a vehicle through which readers can attain and understand their authors' written ideas.

While learning to read, most people are urged to use the dictionary and distinguish words from multiple entries. We help readers skip this step by providing the proper translation based on the surrounding context. In so doing, readers have the chance to invest energy and time in understanding the text and learning vocabulary; they read quickly and easily like a skilled horseman cantering through a book.

Thereby we stress the fact that our proposal is not new at all. Others have tried the same before, coming up with evident and substantial outcomes. Certainly, we are not pioneers in designing interlinear texts. Nonetheless, we are nowadays the only, and doubtless, the best, in providing you with interlinear foreign language texts.

Handling instructions

Using this book is very easy. Each text should be read at least three times in order to explore the whole potential of the method. The first phase is devoted to comparing words in the foreign language to those in the mother tongue. This is to say, the upper line is contrasted to the lower line as the following example shows:

کسان،	اس	کی	بیوی	اور	کھلا	ہوا	دروازہ
(The) peasant	him	to	wife	and	(the) open	being	door
	his				the open door		

The second phase of reading focuses on capturing the meaning and sense of the original text. As readers gain practice with the method, they should be able to focus on the target language without getting distracted by the translation. New users of the method, however, may find it helpful to cover the translated lines with a piece of paper as illustrated in the image below. Subsequently, they try to understand the meaning of every word, phrase, and entire sentences in the target language itself, drawing on the translation only when necessary. In this phase, the reader should resist the temptation to look at the translation for every word. In doing so, they will find that they are able to understand a good portion of the text by reading directly in the target language, without the crutch of the translation. This is the skill we are looking to train: the ability to read and understand native materials and enjoy them as native speakers do, that being, directly in the original language.

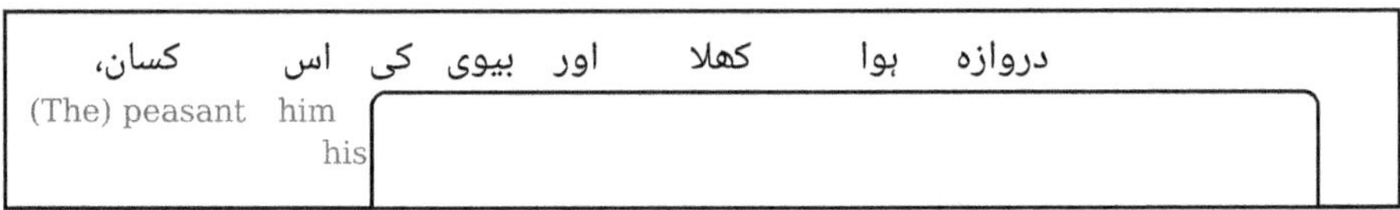

In the final phase, readers will be able to understand the meaning of the text when reading it without additional help. There may be some less common words and phrases which have not cemented themselves yet in the reader's brain, but the majority of the story should not pose any problems. If desired, the reader can use an SRS or some other memorization method to learning these straggling words.

دروازہ ہوا کھلا اور بیوی کی اس کسان،

Above all, readers will not have to look every word up in a dictionary to read a text in the foreign language. This otherwise wasted time will be spent concentrating on their principal interest. These new readers will tackle authentic texts while learning their vocabulary and expressions to use in further communicative (written or oral) situations. This book is just one work from an overall series with the same purpose. It really helps those who are afraid of having "poor vocabulary" to feel confident about reading directly in the language. To all of them and to all of you, welcome to the amazing experience of living a foreign language!

Additional tools

Check out shop.hyplern.com or contact us at info@hyplern.com for free mp3s (if available) and free empty (untranslated) versions of the eBooks that we have on offer.

For some of the older eBooks and paperbacks we have Windows, iOS and Android apps available that, next to the interlinear format, allow for a pop-up format, where hovering over a word or clicking on it gives you its meaning. The apps also have any mp3s, if available, and integrated vocabulary practice.

Visit the site hyplern.com for the same functionality online. This is where we will be working non-stop to make all our material available in multiple formats, including audio where available, and vocabulary practice.

Table of Contents

لالچی بندر

Greedy Monkey (The)

Bandar	Laalchi
بندر	لالچی
Monkey	Greedy (The)

ke	khane	jo	bandar	ek	hai	baat	ki	bar	Ek
کی	کھانے	جو	بندر	ایک	ہے	بات	کی	بار	ایک
for	food	who	monkey	a	is	thing (a)	at	time	One
					there was			Once	

tha	raha	ghum	udhar	idhar	men	talaash
تھا۔	رہا	گھوم	ادھر	ادھر	میں	تلاش
was	being	roaming	here	here	in	searching
			and there			

men	ched	se	chote	andar	ke	chattaan	ek	Use
میں	چھید	سے	چھوٹے	اندر	کے	چٹان	ایک	اسے
in	hole	from	small	inside	of	rock	a	Him
		a small hole						

diye	dikhayi	danen	kuch	ke	gheehon
دیے۔	دکھائی	دانیں	کچھ	کے	گیہوں
gave	see	grains	some	of	wheat
	saw		some grains of wheat		

ko	muthi	apni	aur	dala	andar	haath	apna	ne	Is
کو	مٹھی	اپنی	اور	ڈالا	اندر	ہاتھ	اپنا	نے	اس
-to-	fist	his	and	thrust	enter	hand	his	by	Him
				stuck in				He	

liya bhar se daano
دانوں سے بھر لیا۔
took full with grain
full with grain grabbed

vuh ki tha chota itna sorakh se badqsamti lekin
لیکن بدقسمتی سے سوراخ اتنا چھوٹا تھا کی وہ
he that was small so opening (the) with unfortunate But
unfortunately

saka nikaal nahin muthi apni
اپنی مٹھی نہیں نکال سکا۔
could pull out not fist his

kholna muthi apni vuh ke tha laalchi itna Bandar
بندر اتنا لالچی تھا کہ وہ اپنی مٹھی کھولنا
open fist his he that was greedy so monkey (The)

tha chahta nahin hi
ہی نہیں چاہتا تھا۔
was wanting not even
wanted not even

se kame dheeli muthi ke tha dar ko is Kyunkay
کیونکہ اس کو ڈر تھا کے مٹھی ڈھیلی کرنے سے
of do loose fist that was fear to him Because
by loosening his fist he was afraid

ge jayen ho kam danen
دانیں کم ہو جائیں گے۔
would go is few grain
would spill some grain

nikalna	bahar	bana	kiye	dheeli	ko	muthi	Lekin
نکالنا	باہر	بنا	کیے	ڈھیلی	کو	مٹھی	لیکن
pull	out	make	without	loose	to	fist	But
pulling (it) out		without loosening (it)			his fist		

tha	nahin	asan
تھا۔	نہیں	آسان
was	not	easy
wasn't easy		

nahin	kam	to	danen	ke	gheehon	ne	bandar	laalchi
نہیں	کم	تو	دانیں	کے	گیہوں	نے	بندر	لالچی
not	few	so	grains	of	wheat	by	monkey	greedy (The)
			the grains of wheat					

kiye
کیے۔
done

aur	liya	nikaal	khaali	hi	haath	poora	apna	Albata
اور	لیا	نکال	خالی	ہی	ہاتھ	پورا	اپنا	البتہ
and	take	remove	free	just	hand	whole	his	Consequently
	took out (he)							

gaya	chala	se	vahan	hi	bhooka
گیا۔	چلا	سے	وہاں	ہی	بھوکا
went	move	from	there	just	hungry

4

رنگ برنگا گیدڑ

Color Colored Jackal (The Painted Jackal)

Geedar	Biranga	Rang
گیدڑ	برنگا	رنگ
Jackal	Spotted	Paint (The)
	The Painted Jackal	

ek	vuh	lekin	tha	raha	ghum	talaash	ki	shikaar	geedar	Ek
ایک	وہ	لیکن	تھا	رہا	گھوم	تلاش	کی	شکار	گیدڑ	ایک
a	he	but	was	being	roam	search	to	hunt	jackal	A
				was roaming			searching prey			

jo	gaya	gar	men	matke	se	bare
جو	گیا	گر	میں	مٹکے	سے	بڑے
which	went	fall	in	vat	-of-	large
	fell					

to	pahuncha	ghar	vuh	Jab	tha	hui	bhara	se	rang
تو	پہنچا	گھر	وہ	جب	تھا۔	ہوا	بھرا	سے	رنگ
then	arrived	house	he	When	was	been	full	of	paint
		home					was full of paint		

kar	dekh	men	haalat	is	use	dost	ke	is
کر	دیکھ	میں	حالت	اس	اسے	دوست	کے	اس
did	see	in	state	that	him to	friend(s)	to	him
	seeing							his

aakhir poocha se is ne unhon aur gaye ho heran
حیران ہو گئے اور انہوں نے اس سے پوچھا "آخر
Finally asked of him by them and went is surprise
were surprised

waqua rangeen sa kon sath tumahray hai kya majaarah
ماجرہ کیا ہے، تمہارے ساتھ کون سا رنگین واقعہ
incident colorful of which with you is what affair
colorful incident what with you

ho rahe ghum kar ban rangeele jo gaya aa paish
پیش آ گیا جو رنگیلے بن کر گھوم رہے ہو؟"
is being roam did make colorful which went come before
while roaming made you colorful happened

diya jawab ho mortai ko ponch apni ne Is
اس نے اپنی پونچھ کو موڑتے ہو جواب دیا
gave answer is curling -to- tail his by Him
he answered curled while He

se mujh jo hai cheez koi aisi men duniya
"دنیا میں ایسی کوئی چیز ہے جو مجھ سے
of me which is thing what such in World
than anything In the world

baad ke aaj dekho taraf Meri ho achi ziyada
زیادہ اچھی ہو۔ میری طرف دیکھو، آج کے بعد
after from today look direction My is good more
starting from today better

ga kahe nahin gheedar bhi koi mujhe
مجھے کوئی بھی گیدڑ نہیں کہے گا۔"
will say not jackal also what me
call some

aap	baad	ke	aaj	to	poocha	ne	sathiyon	ke	Is
آپ	بعد	کے	آج	"تو	پوچھا	نے	ساتھیوں	کے	اس
you	after	-to-	today	Then	asked	-by-	friends	to	Him
									His

ga	jaye	kaha	kya	ko
گا۔"	جائے	کہا	کیا	کو
will	go	say	what	-to-
	should call			

baad	ke	aaj	diya	jawab	ne	Geedar
بعد	کے	"آج	دیا	جواب	نے	گیدڑ
after	-to-	Today	gave	answer	by	jackal (The)

ge	bulaao	kar	ke	more	mujhe	log	sabhi	tum
گے۔"	بلاؤ	کر	کہ	مور	مجھے	لوگ	سبھی	تم
will	name (call)	do	say	peacock	me to	people	all	you
							all you people	

sahib	geedar	baad	ke	kehnay	yeh	Aur
صاحب	گیدڑ	بعد	کے	کہنے	یہ	اور
lordly	jackal (the)	after	-to-	to say	this	And

hue	maartay	cholanaghe	neechay	ke	aasman	khulay
ہوئے	مارتے	چھلانگے	نیچے	کے	آسمان	کھلے
was	powerful	leap	under	to	sky	open
				in the open		

lagey	itranay
لگے۔	اترانے
applied	showing off

ne doston ke geedar kar sun ko jawab is ke Is

اس کے اس جواب کو سن کر گیدڑ کے دوستوں نے

by friend(s) to jackal do hear -to- answer his to This

to the Jackal hearing

bohat to ponch ki more ke poocha se is

اس سے پوچھا کہ مور کی پونچھ تو بہت

very then tail (the) to peacock (the) -to- asked from him

to the peacock

to hai phelata usay woh jab hai hoti shandaar hi

ہی شاندار ہوتی ہے جب وہ اسے پھیلاتا ہے تو

then is spread it that when is being beautiful -so-

kya hai karta paish manzar se khobsorat hi bohat

بہت ہی خوبصورت سے منظر پیش کرتا ہے کیا

what is doing before view from beautiful so much

so

hai kamaal yeh bhi men ponch ki aap

آپ کی پونچھ میں بھی یہ کمال ہے؟

is great this also in tail to you

the tail with you

bhi bilkul aisa to vuh ke diya jawab ne Geedar

گیدڑ نے جواب دیا کہ وہ تو ایسا بالکل بھی

also much so then he that gave answer by Jackal (The)

sakta kar nahin

نہیں کر سکتا۔

could do not

aawaz more jab ke bataya use ne doston ke Is
اس کے دوستوں نے اسے بتایا کہ جب مور آواز
voice peacock when to told him by friend(s) to Him

hai hofti mithaas ek men awaaz ki is to hai nikalta
نکالتا ہے تو اس کی آواز میں ایک مٹھاس ہوتی ہے
is was sweet one in voice to him then is brought

nikaal awaaz aisi bhi vuh kya ke poocha se is aur
اور اس سے پوچھا کہ کیا وہ بھی ایسی آواز نکال
bring voice such also he what to ask from him and

hai sakta
سکتا ہے؟
is could

yeh ke kaha ne geedar niqalchi bewaqoof is par Is
اس پر اس بیوقوف نقلچی گیدڑ نے کہا کہ یہ
this that say by jackal pretender foolish this on This
Then

bhi bilkul aisa men ke gi pari manni to baat
بات تو ماننی پڑی گی کہ میں ایسا بالکل بھی
also much such I that will had to accept then thing
so you will have to accept

sakta kar nahin
نہیں کر سکتا۔
could do not
can do

baat yeh jab ke kaha se is ne doston ke is To
تو اس کے دوستوں نے اس سے کہا کہ جب یہ بات
thing this when that said of him by friends to him Then
to him his

nah aur ho geedar to nah tum ke gayi ho saaf
صاف ہو گئی کہ تم نہ تو گیدڑ ہو اور نہ
not and are jackal then neither you that went be clear
is

sath hamare tum to ho sakte ban more tum hi
ہی تم مور بن سکتے ہو تو تم ہمارے ساتھ
with us you then be could do peacock you either
with us can be

use ne doston ke is terhan is Aur ho rahe kar kya
کیا کر رہے ہو؟ اور اس طرح اس کے دوستوں نے اسے
him by friend(s) to him at this And is being do what
his are doing

diya nikaal se baradri apni
اپنی برادری سے نکال دیا۔
did bring from community their

کسان، اس کی بیوی اور کھلا ہوا دروازہ

The Peasant, his Wife and the Open Door

darwaazah hua khula aur biwi ki us Kisaan

کسان، اس کی بیوی اور کھلا ہوا دروازہ

door being open (the) and wife to him peasant (The)

the open door his

ke biwi apni kisaan ghareeb ek hai baat ki baar Ek

یک بار کی بات ہے ایک غریب کسان اپنی بیوی کے

to wife his peasant poor a is thing at time One

Once there was

apna aur karne khatam kaam ka bhar din sath

ساتھ دن بھر کا کام ختم کرنے اور اپنا

their and do finish work of full day with

finished

baithe paas ke aag baad ke khane khana sa mamooli

معمولی سا کھانا کھانے کے بعد آگ کے پاس بیٹھے

sit down by of fire after of to eat meal of ordinary

by the fire simple meal

ke un achanak lekin thei rahe kar aram thora hue

ہوئے تھوڑا آرام کر رہے تھے لیکن اچانک ان کے

of them suddenly but were stay do comfort a little were

them were resting

kon darwaazah ke gayi ho larai par baat is beech
بیچ اس بات پر لڑائی ہو گئی کہ دروازہ کون
who the door that went is fight on thing this between
has come up

se jhonke taiz ke hua kyunkei ga kere band
بند کرے گا کیونکہ ہوا کے تیز جھونکے سے
from gust (wind) sharp of happened because will do close
by a strong gust of wind will close

tha gaya khul pura darwaazah
دروازہ پورا کھل گیا تھا۔
was went open whole the door
blown wide

darwaazah ho sunthee kaha se biwi apni ne Aadmi
آدمی نے اپنی بیوی سے کہا "سنتی ہو دروازہ
the door is listen said of wife own by man (The)
to his

do kar band
بند کر دو"
give do close
shut

khud tum ho sunthe kaha men jawab ne Aurat
عورت نے جواب میں کہا "سنتے ہو تم خود
self(your) you is Listen said in reply by woman (The)
Listen

dele kar nahin kyun band use hi
ہی اسے بند کیوں نہیں کر دیتے"۔
give do not why close it just
don't you

karogi band darwaaza tum nah Agar kaha ne Shohar

شوہر نے کہا "اگر نہ تم دروازہ بند کروگی

will do close door (the) you not If said -by- husband (The)

kaam Ek ga kare band kaun darwaazah to men nah aur

اور نہ میں تو دروازہ کون بند کرے گا؟ ایک کام

task One will do close no one door (the) so I not and

will close

wuhi ga bolay pehlay bhi jo tak subah hain karte

کرتے ہیں صبح تک جو بھی پہلے بولے گا وہی

same will speak first also who up to morning are do

that one will speak from the morning let's do

ga kare band darwaazah

دروازہ بند کرے گا"۔

will do close door (the)

will close

vuh aur lagi achi bahut ko biwi ki us baat Yih

یہ بات اس کی بیوی کو بہت اچھی لگی اور وہ

she and look good very to wife to him thing This

seemed his

par bistar apne hi kahe kuch bana khushi khushi

خوشی خوشی بنا کچھ کہے ہی اپنے بستر پر

on bed their without speak some make happiness happiness

{نہیں} very happy

gayi chali sonay

سونے چلی گئی۔

went go sleep

went

diya sunai shor kuch unhen ko raat Aadhi
آدھی رات کو انہیں کچھ شور سنائی دیا
gave listen noise some them to night Halfway
In the middle of the night

to dekha kar jihaank bahar se bistar apne ne unhon jab
جب انہوں نے اپنے بستر سے باہر جھانک کر دیکھا تو
so look do look out from bed their by them when

ghis men ghar kutta jungli ek ke hua ehsas unhen
انہیں احساس ہوا کہ ایک جنگلی کتا گھر میں گھس
enter in home dog wild a that was sensed them

ko khane hue bache se thore ke un jo hai aaya
آیا ہے جو ان کے تھوڑے سے بچے ہوئے کھانے کو
to food done remain from little of them who is came
leftover their

men logon bewaqoof hi Donon hai raha kar harap
ہڑپ کر رہا ہے۔ دونوں ہی بیوقوف لوگوں میں
in people silly just Both of them is being do devour
being was

har ne kutte aur bola nahin kuch bhi koi se
سے کوئی بھی کچھ نہیں بولا اور کتے نے ہر
every by dogs and talked not some also someone from
didn't say anything

bhar pet tha sakta kha jo bad ke sunghnay ko cheez
چیز کو سونگھنے کے بعد جو کھا سکتا تھا پیٹ بھر
full belly was can eat who after of sniff to thing

gaya chala bahar se ghar aur khaya kar
کر کھایا اور گھر سے باہر چلا گیا۔
went move out from home and ate do

men chuki gheehon se thore aurat roz Agle
اگلے روز عورت تھوڑے سے گیہوں چکی میں
in took wheat from little (a) woman (the) day next (The)
took a little wheat

gayi le ghar ke parosi liye ke shavaane
پسوانے کے لئے پڑوسی کے گھر لے گئی۔
went take home of neighbor for to grinding
at the neighbor's house to grind

gayi ghar ke parosi shavaane geehoon aurat wuh Jab
جب وہ عورت گیہوں پسوانے پڑوسی کے گھر گئی
went home of neighbor grinding wheat woman this When

to aaya ghar ke us naai ek tabhi
تبھی ایک نائی اس کے گھر آیا تو
so came home of her barber a then

baithy kyun akaile Aj bola se shohar ke us
اس کے شوہر سے بولا "آج اکیلے کیوں بیٹھے
sit down why alone Today spoke from husband of her
to her husband

ho
ہو؟"
are you

ne Naai diya nahin jawab koi ne Kisaan
کسان نے کوئی جواب نہیں دیا۔ نائی نے
by barber (The) gave not reply any by farmer (The)
The barber did not reply anything The farmer

phir wuh lekin kiye saaf ke sar ke bal is
اس بال کے سر کے صاف کیے لیکن وہ پھر
then he but did clear of hair of head him
shaved half his head half his head

ki kisaan ne naai Tab bola nahin kuch bhi
بھی کچھ نہیں بولا۔ تب نائی نے کسان کی
to farmer (the) by barber (the) Then said not some also
anything

di kar saaf moonch aadhi aur daarhi aadhi
آدھی داڑھی اور آدھی مونچھ صاف کر دی
gave do clear mustache (the) half and beard (the) half
shaved

ke Is raha khamosh bhi phir kisaan bewaqoof lekin
لیکن بیوقوف کسان پھر بھی خاموش رہا۔ اس کے
of Him remained quiet also then farmer foolish (the) but

par jism pura ke is ne naai baad
بعد نائی نے اس کے پورے جسم پر
on body entire of him by barber after
whole body his by the barber

kisaan wuh lekin di mil kalak se tarah bari hi bahut
بہت ہی بری طرح سے کالک مل دی لیکن وہ کسان
farmer this but gave rub soot from like bad just very
soot rubbed a lot of

ho murat koi ki pathar ki jaise raha bana aisa

ایسا بنا رہا جیسے کی پتھر کی کوئی مورت ہو۔

is statue some of stone to like remaining do such

remained

ke diya kar shuru chalana ne naai is Tab

تب اس نائی نے چلانا شروع کر دیا کہ

that gave do start to exclaim by barber this Then

exclaimed

ghabaraakar aur hai gaya aa bhoot par aadmi is

اس آدمی پر بھوت آ گیا ہے اور گھبراکر

panic and is went come ghost (a) on man this

in panicked became this man

hua khara bhaag se ghar se jaldi

جلدی سے گھر سے بھاگ کھڑا ہوا۔

was standing ran from home with haste

ranfrom the home haste

se ghar naai to looti biwi Jab

جب بیوی لوٹی تو نائی گھر سے

from home barber then returned wife (the) When

bari itni ko shohar apne ne is jab tha chuka ja

جا چکا تھا جب اس نے اپنے شوہر کو اتنی بری

bad so much to husband her by her when was done go

had gone

se munh ke is kar ghabra to dekha men halaat

حالت میں دیکھا تو گھبرا کر اس کے مونھ سے

from mouth of her do panic so see in condition

{مُنہ}

ho rahe kar kya tum Yih nikla

نکلا "یہ تم کیا کر رہے ہو؟"

are you ing- do what you this came out

Aur bolein pahle Tum chalaya se khoshi Kisaan

کسان خوشی سے چلایا "تم پہلے بولیں"۔ اور

And speak first You exclaims from happiness farmer (The)

para karna band darwaaza ko aurat is tarah is

اس طرح اس عورت کو دروازہ بند کرنا پڑا۔

had to to do close the door to woman his like this

بینور کے سات عقلمند آدمی

The Seven Wise Men of Buneyr

admi	aqqelmand	sat	ke	benor
آدمی	عقلمند	سات	کے	بینور
men (The)	wise	seven	of	Benor
	The seven wise men of Buneyr			

ki	karoobar	admi	aqqelmand	sat	ke	Benor	bar	Ek
کی	کاروبار	آدمی	عقلمند	سات	کے	بینور	بار	ایک
to	work	men	wisdom-full	seven	of	Benor	time	One
			wise					

nikal	kar	chor	ko	jangl	fedaishi	apne	men	talash
نکل	کر	چھوڑ	کو	جنگل	پیدائشی	اپنے	میں	تلاش
get out	do	leave	to	forest	native	their	in	search
	leaving							

neeche	ke	fir	ek	sabhi	vuh	vaqt	ke	Sham	paddi
نیچے	کے	پیڑ	ایک	سبھی	وہ	وقت	کے	شام	پڑے۔
under	of	tree	a	all	they	time	of	Evening	get down
						In the evening			

ek	se	men	in	tabhi	ghay	beth	liye	ke	karne	aram
ایک	سے	میں	ان	تبھی	گئے	بیٹھ	لئے	کے	کرنے	آرام
one	from	in	them	then	went	sit	for	of	do	comfort
		from them			sat				to rest	

se	men	ham	ke	lyen	kar	ghinti	bar	Ek	bola	admi
سے	میں	ہم	کہ	لیں	کر	گنتی	بار	"ایک	بولا	آدمی
from	in	we	that	take	do	counting	time	One	spoke	man
from ourselves					let's count					

ghinnaa ne us lye Is ghayaa ho nahin to kam koyi
کوئی کم تو نہیں ہو گیا۔" اس لئے اس نے گننا
counting by him for Him went is not then less what
missing someone

vuh Lekin che pansh char tin do Ek kya sharoo
شروع کیا۔ "ایک، دو، تین، چار، پانچ، چھ"۔ لیکن وہ
this but six five four three two One did start

zor Vuh gheya bhol ghinnaa ko xud admi aqqelmand
عقلمند آدمی خود کو گننا بھول گیا۔ وہ زور
force He went forget counting to self man wisdom-full
wise

hai kam ek men Ham bola aur chilaya se
سے چلّایا اور بولا "ہم میں ایک کم ہے!"
is less one in We said and exclaimed with
Of us

ne logon Saton vaquf be chilay log Dusre
دوسرے لوگ چلّائے "بے وقوف!" ساتوں لوگوں نے
by people seven (The) sense -Non exclaimed men other (The)

ko dusre ek athakur ungli ke kar ek bad ke ek
ایک کے بعد ایک کر کے انگلی اٹھاکر ایک دوسرے کو
to other -an get up finger to do one after to one
with a raised finger one after one

ek har se men in lekin kya sharoo ghinnaa
گننا شروع کیا لیکن ان میں سے ہر ایک
one every from in they but did start count
from them

gheya	bhol	ghinnaa	ko	xud
گیا۔	بھول	گننا	کو	خود
went	forget	count	to	selves(them)
	forgot			

afit	burri	koyi	jaise	laga	aisa	unhen
آفت	بری	کوئی	جیسے	لگا	ایسا	انہیں
disaster	bad	some	like	felt	such	To them
					this	

ho	kharree	hi	fora	Vuh	ho	aadhumki	par	in
ہو	کھڑے	ہی	فورا	وہ	ہو۔	آدھمکی	پر	ان
is	upright	just	immediately	They	is	come-threat	on	them
						had come upon them		

lagi	karne	talash	ko	saathi	saatven	apne	aur	ghey
لگے۔	کرنے	تلاش	کو	ساتھی	ساتویں	اپنے	اور	گئے
take	do	search	to	companion	seventh	their	and	went

ne	jis	mile	se	chervahe	ek	vuh	bad	deer	Thori
نے	جس	ملے	سے	چرواہے	ایک	وہ	بعد	دیر	تھوڑی
by	which	meet	from	shepherd	a	them	after	while	little (A)

ki	bat	se	tarah	achhi	bahut	aur	kya	salaam	inhen
کی۔	بات	سے	طرح	اچھی	بہت	اور	کیا	سلام	انہیں
did	thing	from	like	good	very	and	did	greeting	them

log	sabhi	ap	Doston	poocha	se	un	Aur
لوگ	سبھی	آپ	"دوستوں،	پوچھا۔	سے	ان	اور
people	all	you	Friends	asks	from	them	And

ho rahe de dekhaye kyon mayoos itne
اتنے مایوس کیوں دکھائی دے رہے ہو؟"
is being give see why despondent so much
are looking

dost ek Hamaara deeya javab sath ek ne Inhoon
انہوں نے ایک ساتھ جواب دیا "ہمارا ایک دوست
friend one Our gave answer with one by Them
They all as

to thay chalee log ham subhe Jab hai geya kho
کھو گیا ہے۔ جب صبح ہم لوگ چلے تھے تو
then were go people we morning When is went lose
got lost

Kya hain hi chay sirf ham ab lekin thay sat ham
ہم سات تھے لیکن اب ہم صرف چھ ہی ہیں۔ کیا
What are just six only we now but were seven we

hai dekha ko kaysi pas as yahahn ne ap
آپ نے یہاں آس پاس کسی کو دیکھا ہے؟"
is see to someone by near here by you
someone saw around

Dekho ho tum satven Lekin kya javaab ne chervahe Is
اس چرواہے نے جواب دیا "لیکن ساتویں تم ہو۔ دیکھو
Look is you seven But gave answer by shepherd This

tumhara ne Men sat aur che panch char tin do ek
ایک، دو، تین، چار، پانچ، چھ اور سات! میں نے تمہارا
your by Me seven and six five four three two one

hai liya kar talash saathi satvaan
ساتواں ساتھی تلاش کر لیا ہے۔"
is took do search companion seventh
was found

Ap diya javab ne admion aqqelmand sathon ke Benoor
بینور کے ساتوں عقلمند آدمیوں نے جواب دیا۔ "آپ
You gave answer by men wise seven of Benor (The)

karne talash ko sathi satven hamare yaqeena ne
نے یقینا ہمارے ساتویں ساتھی کو تلاش کرکے
doing search to companion seventh our indeed by
finding

bahut ke ap Ham hai ki madar kafi hamari
ہماری کافی مدد کی ہے۔ ہم آپ کے بہت
very to you We is to help enough us
a lot of

hai kiya kam bara bahut hamara ne Ap hain guzar shukr
شکر گزار ہیں۔ آپ نے ہمارا بہت بڑا کام کیا ہے۔
is did work great very to us by You are paying thanks
thankful

karen kam men moft mahina ek liye ke ap ham liye Is
اس لئے ہم آپ کے لئے ایک مہینہ مفت میں کام کریں
do work in free month one for of you we for This

ge
گے۔"
will

apne	unhin	sath	apne	aur	hua	xush	bahut	Chervaha
اپنے	انہیں	ساتھ	اپنے	اور	ہوا	خوش	بہت	چرواہا
his	them	with	himself	and	was	happy	very	shepherd (The)

gaya	le	ghar
گیا۔	لے	گھر
went	take	home

Vuh	thi	gayi	ho	boodhi	bahut	mahn	ki	Chervahe
وہ	تھی۔	گئی	ہو	بوڑھی	بہت	ماں	کی	چرواہے
She	was	went	is	old	very	mother	to	shepherd (The)

ho	bahut	bhi	kamzor	aur	thi	gayi	bhi	sathya
ہو	بہت	بھی	کمزور	اور	تھی	گئی	بھی	سٹھیا
is	very	also	weak	and	was	went	also	in her dotage

ke	thi	nahin	taqut	bhi	itni	men	Is	thi	gayi
کہ	تھی	نہیں	طاقت	بھی	اتنی	میں	اس	تھی۔	گئی
that	was	not	strength	also	so much	in	Her	was	went

hone	Sabha	sake	kar	se	asani	kam	koyi	apna
ہونے	صبح	سکے۔	کر	سے	آسانی	کام	کوئی	اپنا
to be	morning (The)	could	do	from	ease	work	any	her

admi	ek	ke	benor	ko	mahn	apni	ne	chervahe	is	par
آدمی	ایک	کے	بینور	کو	ماں	اپنی	نے	چرواہے	اس	پر
man	one	of	benor	to	mother	his	by	shepherd	this	on

mahn	meri	Tum	kaha	se	is	aur	dya	men	xidmat	ki
ماں	میری	"تم	کہا	سے	اس	اور	دیا	میں	خدمت	کی
mother	my	You	said	to	him	and	gave	in	service	to

ge rakho dihan ka un aur ge raho pas ke
کے پاس رہو گے اور ان کا دھیان رکھو گے۔"
will keep attention to her and will stay by to

men din vuh ki kaha ne us se admi Dusre
دوسرے آدمی سے اس نے کہا کہ وہ دن میں
in day they that said by him from man other (The)
He told the other man

aur ga jaye le charaane par pahari ko bakryon ki is
اس کی بکریوں کو پہاڑی پر چرانے لے جائے گا اور
and will go take to pasture on hill to goats to he
his

admyon panchon aur ga kare hefazat ki in men rat
رات میں ان کی حفاظت کرے گا اور پانچوں آدمیوں
men five and will do safety to them in night
should guard

karne kam roz agle sath ke is vuh ke kaha se
سے کہا کہ وہ اس کے ساتھ اگلے روز کام کرنے
do work day next (the) with to him they that said from

ge jaen
جائیں گے۔
would go

ghar liye ke xidmat ki mahn ki us jo admi Vuh
وہ آدمی جو اس کی ماں کی خدمت کے لئے گھر
home for of service to mother to him who man That
his

Gharmi	raha	arata	ko	Makhion	bhar	din	tha	raka	par
گرمی	رہا۔	اڑاتا	کو	مکھیوں	بھر	دن	تھا	رکا	پر
heat (The)	stayed	to fan	to	flies	full	day	was	stop	on
								remained	

boorhi	is	bar	bar	makhion	aur	thi	ziyadah	bahut
بوڑھی	اس	بار	بار	مکھیاں	اور	تھی	زیادہ	بہت
old	this	time	time	flies (the)	and	was	excessive	very

tarah	is	ke	laga	Usse	thihn	jati	baith	akar	par	aurat
طرح	اس	کہ	لگا	اسے	تھیں۔	جاتی	بیٹھ	آکر	پر	عورت
like	this	that	felt	He	were	going	sit	will	on	woman
way										

usse	hoga	nahin	faida	koyi	se	arane	ko	makhion
اسے	ہوگا	نہیں	فائدہ	کوئی	سے	اڑانے	کو	مکھیوں
to him	will be	not	benefit	any	from	to fan	to	flies

ne	kyon	ki	socha	ne	Us	hoga	karna	aur	kooch
نہ	کیوں	کہ	سوچا	نے	اس	ہوگا۔	کرنا	اور	کچھ
not	why	that	thought	by	Him	will be	to do	and	some

us	kar	sooch	Yih	jaye	mara	se	pathar	ko	makhion
اس	کر	سوچ	یہ	جائے۔	مارا	سے	پتھر	کو	مکھیوں
him	do	thinking	This	go	hit	from	stone	to	flies (the)

par	makhi	ek	aur	uthaya	pathar	sa	bara	ek	ne
پر	مکھی	ایک	اور	اٹھایا	پتھر	سا	بڑا	ایک	نے
at	fly	a	and	picked up	stone	of	great	a	by

ek	pathar	vuh	se	taqut	puri	ne	Us	lagaya	neshana
ایک	پتھر	وہ	سے	طاقت	پوری	نے	اس	لگایا۔	نشانا
one	stone	this	with	force	full	by	Him	applied	aim

sathi	par	sar	ke	aurat	is	jo	mara	de	par	makhi
بیٹھی	پر	سر	کے	عورت	اس	جو	مارا	دے	پر	مکھی
sit down	on	head	of	woman	this	which	hit	give	on	fly

to	mara	pathar	ne	us	jab	Lekin	thi	hui
تو	مارا	پتھر	نے	اس	جب	لیکن	تھی۔	ہوئی
then	hit	stone (the)	by	him	when	But	was	happened

lekin	gayi	ar	se	vahan	sath	ke	sakon	makhi
لیکن	گئی	اڑ	سے	وہاں	ساتھ	کے	سکون	مکھی
but	went	flew	from	there	with	to	easily	fly (the)
		away flew						

vapas	chervaha	Jab	laga	ko	aurat	is	pather
واپس	چرواہا	جب	لگا۔	کو	عورت	اس	پتھر
back	shepherd (the)	When	apply	to	woman	this	stone (the)
			struck				

pat	lat	se	xun	ko	mahn	apni	aur	lota
پت	لت	سے	خون	کو	ماں	اپنی	اور	لوٹا
-	smeared	from	blood	to	mother	his	and	returned
completely covered								

hua	afsoos	bahut	par	faisla	apne	usse	to	dekha
ہوا	افسوس	بہت	پر	فیصلہ	اپنے	اسے	تو	دیکھا
was	sorry	very	on	decision	his own	to him	then	saw

Makhi	kiya	kya	yih	ne	bevakhoofi	Teri	challaya	aur
مکھی	کیا؟	کیا	یہ	نے	بیوقوفی	"تیری	چلّایا	اور
fly (The)	did	what	this	by	stupidity	Your	exclaimed	and

dalla mar ko mahn meri ne to lekin gayi ar to
تو اڑ گئی لیکن تو نے میری ماں کو مار ڈالا۔"
put kill to mother my by then but went fly then
did

ke bakryon ke us admi benoori dusra dooran Issi
اسی دوران دوسرا بینوری آدمی اس کے بکریوں کے
of goats to him man Benory the second during That
Meanwhile

din adha aur raha hankta udhar idhar par pahari ko reever
ریوڑ کو پہاڑی پر ادھر ادھر ہانکتا رہا اور آدھا دن
day half and being drive there here on hill to herd
urge on

apna aur gaya baith liye ke karne aram par ghuzarne
گزرنے پر آرام کرنے کے لئے بیٹھ گیا اور اپنا
his and went sit for of do comfort on passing

bhi bakryon kuch hi qarib ke Is laga khane khana
کھانا کھانے لگا۔ اس کے قریب ہی کچھ بکریاں بھی
also goats some just close of This apply eat meal
- ate

ghayen baith liye ke karne aram
آرام کرنے کے لئے بیٹھ گئیں۔
went (they) sit for of do comfort

dekha ne us to tha raha kha khana apna vuh Jab
جب وہ اپنا کھانا کھا رہا تھا تو اس نے دیکھا
saw by him then was being eat meal his he When

dekh taraf ki us vaqt karte jugali bakryon ke
کہ بکریاں جگالی کرتے وقت اس کی طرف دیکھ
look direction of him while do rumination goats that
- chew the cud

mazaq ka us vuh ke soocha ne Us thin rahi
رہی تھیں۔ اس نے سوچا کہ وہ اس کا مزاق
joke of him they that thought by Him were (they) being

ho naraaz vuh kar soch yahi aur hain rahi ora
اڑا رہی ہیں اور یہی سوچ کر وہ ناراض ہو
is angry he do thinking like that and are being blow

khana apna Main kahaa se in kar chalaa ne Us gheeya
گیا۔ اس نے چلا کر ان سے کہا "میں اپنا کھانا
meal my I said from them do move by Him went

rahi ara mazaaq mera log tum aur hoon raha kha
کھا رہا ہوں اور تم لوگ میرا مزاق اڑا رہی
being blow joke (a) me to people you and am being eat

se kolhari choti ek ne us kar kaha Yih ho
ہو۔"۔ یہ کہہ کر اس نے ایک چھوٹی کلہاڑی سے
with ax small a by him do saying This is

diya kar sharoo karna hamla par janoron masoom un
ان معصوم جانوروں پر حملہ کرنا شروع کر دیا۔
gave do start to do attack on animals innocent those

is ke dekha ne us to aya vahan chervaha Jab
جب چرواہا وہاں آیا تو اس نے دیکھا کہ اس
this that saw by him then came there shepherd (the) When

admi bevaquf Is hain pari mari bakryan si bahut ki
کی بہت سی بکریاں مری پڑی ہیں۔ اس بیوقوف آدمی
man foolish This are lay dead goats of many of

thi di kat hi ghardin ki bakryon si bahut ne
نے بہت سی بکریوں کی گردن ہی کاٹ دی تھی۔
was gave cut of neck (the) of goats of many by

is kar chilla ne us hue rote par badnasibi Apni
اپنی بدنصیبی پر روتے ہوئے اس نے چلا کر اس
this do screaming by him being crying on misfortune His

raho baz se am qatal Is kaha se admi
آدمی سے کہا "اس قتل عام سے باز رہو۔"
stay arm from common murder This said to man
stop with

rat hamghin se sab ki chervahi bichare us rat Vuh
وہ رات اس بیچارے چرواہے کی سب سے غمگین رات
night sad from all to shepherd poor this night That

bhi pashtava kafi par bazi jad apni usse aur thi
تھی اور اسے اپنی جلد بازی پر کافی پچھتاوا بھی
also regret enough on bet early his to him and was

hue bachi (baqi) panchon ko Subha tha raha ho
ہو رہا تھا۔ صبح کو پانچوں باقی ہوئے
being remaining five to morning (The) was being is

Ab kaha se is aur aye pas ke us admi aqqelmand
عقلمند آدمی اس کے پاس آئے اور اس سے کہا "اب
Now said to him and came by of him men wise

batayen kam koyi bhi hamen hai bari hamari
ہماری باری ہے ہمیں بھی کوئی کام بتائیں۔"
tell (to do) work what also us is (it) turn our

peyari meri nahin Nahin bola kar ghabra Chervaha
چرواہا گھبرا کر بولا "نہیں، نہیں میرے پیارے
dear my no No talked do panicking shepherd (The)

kar dhund ko sathi hue khoy ke Aap doston
دوستوں۔ آپ کے کھوئے ہوئے ساتھی کو ڈھونڈ کر
do find to companion happened lost got of You friends
- found

aap tha kiya sath ke aap ne main ehsan mamooli jo
جو معمولی احسان میں نے آپ کے ساتھ کیا تھا آپ
you was what with for you by me favor minor (a) which

hai di kar ada hi pahli qimat bari bahut ki is ne
نے اس کی بہت بڑی قیمت پہلے ہی ادا کر دی ہے۔
is gave do pay just first price big very to this by
- paid - already payment

jao chale raste apne se yahan ab liye ke Xuda
خدا کے لئے اب یہاں سے اپنے راستے چلے جاؤ
go let (you) go ways your from here now sake for God

chahta nahin dhekhna bhi surat tumhari main kyonki
کیونکہ میں تمہاری صورت بھی دھیکھنا نہیں چاہتا۔"
want not see also face your I because

aqqelmand saton ke benor bad ke sunne javab Yih
یہ جواب سننے کے بعد بینور کے ساتوں عقلمند
wise seven of Benor after of listen answer This
the Buneyrian

ghaye	ho	ravana	taraf	ki	manzil	nayi	apni	aadmi
گئے۔	ہو	روانہ	طرف	کی	منزل	نئی	اپنی	آدمی
went	is	depart	direction	to	destination	new	their	men

شیر اور خرگوش

The Tiger and the Hare

Khargush	aur	Sher
خرگوش	اور	شیر
hare (the)	and	tiger (The)

sher	khaufnaak	hi	bahut	ek	men	jangal	khaas	Ek
شیر	خوفناک	ہی	بہت	ایک	میں	جنگل	خاص	ایک
tiger	fearsome	very	much	one	in	forest	certain	One

jaanvaron	dusre	hi	liye	ke	khel	sirf	jo	tha	rahta
جانوروں	دوسرے	ہی	لئے	کے	کھیل	صرف	جو	تھا	رہتا
animals	other (the)	just	for	of	game	only	who	was	staying
				for sports					

ya	ho	lagi	bhuk	us	chahe	tha	karta	kiya	shikaar	ka
یا	ہو	لگی	بھوک	اسے	چاہے	تھا	کرتا	کیا	شکار	کا
or	is	apply	hunger	him	whether	was	doing	did	hunt	of

hal	ka	pareeshani	apni	jaanvar	tamaam	liye	Is	nahin
حل	کا	پریشانی	اپنی	جانور	تمام	لئے	اس	نہیں۔
solution	of	problems	their	animals	all	for	This	not

ek	se	raay	ittifaaq	am	liye	ke	karne	talash
ایک	سے	رائے	اتفاق	عام	لئے	کے	کرنے	تلاش
one	from	counsel	agreement	general	for	of	do	search

hue jema jagha

جگہ جمع ہوئے۔

done together place

ho raazee par bat is ham na Kyon kaha ne Geeder

گیدڑ نے کہا "کیوں نہ ہم اس بات پر راضی ہو

is willing on thing this we not Why said by jackal (The)

ke sher hi xud jaanvar ek se men ham ki jayen

جائیں کہ ہم میں سے ایک جانور خود ہی شیر کے

of tiger just self animals one from in we that go

kon pas ke Sher jaaye dene qurbani apni pas

پاس اپنی قربانی دینے جائے۔ شیر کے پاس کون

who by of tiger (The) go give sacrifice his by

hoga se endazi qoora fesla ka us ga jaaye

جائے گا اس کا فیصلہ قرعہ اندازی سے ہوگا۔"

will be from style lottery decision of him will go

ki is ne sabhi aur ayi passand ko sabhi bat Yih

یہ بات سبھی کو پسند آئی اور سبھی نے اس کی

to this by all and came like to all thing This

Everyone liked this

kyon ke ghayi rakhi bhi bat Yih di de manzoori

منظوری دے دی۔ یہ بات بھی رکھی گئی کہ کیوں

why that went put also thing This gave give approval

apni usse aur jaaye jaaya pas ke sher na

نہ شیر کے پاس جایا جائے اور اسے اپنی

their to him and go went by to tiger (the) not

go to

jaye di derhaast
درخواست دی جائے۔
go gave petition

taraf ki ghar ke sher sath ek jaanvar Saaray
سارے جانور ایک ساتھ شیر کے غار کی طرف
direction to cave of tiger (the) with one animals All
together

kaha se is sath ke aajizee hi bahut aur hue ravana
روانہ ہوئے اور بہت ہی عاجزی کے ساتھ اس سے کہا
said to this with of humility very much and be depart
very much departed

parheez se karne shikaar ka janvaar ek har vuh ke
کہ وہ ہر ایک جانور کا شکار کرنے سے پرہیز
avoid from do hunt of animals one every he that

se marzee apni janvaar ek roz har ke kyon kare
کرے کیوں کہ ہر روز ایک جانور اپنی مرضی سے
from choice his animal one day every that why do
out of their own volition because

ga aaye pas ke is
اس کے پاس آئے گا۔
will came by of him
would come to him

gharib hamare Aap ki kaha se is ne Jaanvaron
جانوروں نے اس سے کہا کہ "آپ ہمارے غریب
poor us You that said to this by animals (The)

ke khane ke aap jaanvar Ek karen na shikaar ka satyon
ساتیوں کا شکار نہ کریں۔ ایک جانور آپ کے کھانے کے
of food of you animal one please not hunt of fellows

aap se jis ga kare jaya a hi xud liye
لئے خود ہی آ جایا کرے گا جس سے آپ
you from which will do go come just self for
because of which by themselves

ge jayen bach bhi se pareeshani
پریشانی سے بھی بچ جائیں گے۔"
would go save also from trouble
would be saved hard work

shikaar apna nahin Bilkul chillaya sher kar sun Yih
یہ سن کر شیر چِلّایا "بالکل نہیں، اپنا شکار
hunt my not Absolutely exclaimed tiger do hear This

apna aur ga karon se danton aur panjon apne men
میں اپنے پنجوں اور دانتوں سے کروں گا اور اپنا
my and will do from teeth and claws my in

ga karoon hasil hi xud khana
کھانا خود ہی حاصل کروں گا۔"
will do get just self meal

hamen hai firmaan ka xuda ki diya javab ne Jaanvaron
جانوروں نے جواب دیا کہ خدا کا فرمان ہے ہمیں
us is decree of god that gave answer by animals (The)

chaheeye chorna nahin daamen ka umid
امید کا دامن نہیں چھوڑنا چاہیے۔
should abandon not skirt of hope
take away sliver

ne is lekin hai sahee yih ke diya javab ne Sher
شیر نے جواب دیا کہ یہ صحیح ہے لیکن اس نے
by him but is correct this that gave answer by tiger (The)
(god) answered The tiger

apni koyi har ke hai diya hukum bhi yih
یہ بھی حکم دیا ہے کہ ہر کوئی اپنی
his what every that is gave order also this
everybody

kare talash hi xud rozi
روزی خود ہی تلاش کرے۔
to do search just self provision
must find their own provision

par bat is sher bad ke behas Kafi
کافی بحث کے بعد شیر اس بات پر
on thing this tiger (the) after of discussion Ample
with this After ample discussion

shikaar ka jaanvar kisi vuh aindah ki gaya ho raazee
راضی ہو گیا کہ آئندہ وہ کسی جانور کا شکار
hunt of animal some he next time that went is agreed
agreed

ka jaanvar hi kar ruk men ghar apne aur ga kare nahin
نہیں کرے گا اور اپنے غار میں رک کر ہی جانور کا
of animal just do stay in cave his and will do not
won't

roz har se bad ke Is ga kare intizar
انتظار کرے گا۔ اس کے بعد سے ہر روز
day every from after of This will do to await

kar chun se andaazi khura jaanvar koyi na koyi
کوئی نہ کوئی جانور قرعہ اندازی سے چن کر
do select from manner fate animal what not what
selected by fate some or other

jata diya bhej liye ke sher
شیر کے لئے بھیج دیا جاتا۔
would go gave send for of tiger
would be send to the tiger

aur geya akar vuh to aya vaqt ka xargosh jab Lekin
لیکن جب خرگوش کا وقت آیا تو وہ اکڑ گیا اور
and went strut she then came time of hare (the) when But

aur abhi Main ga jaon nahin pas ke sher Main bola
بولا "میں شیر کے پاس نہیں جاؤں گا۔ میں ابھی اور
more now I will go not by of tiger I spoke

hun chaahta rehna zinda
زندہ رہنا چاہتا ہوں۔"
am wanting remain live
want to

ki koshish bahut ki manaanee us ne jaanvaron Tamaam
تمام جانوروں نے اسے منانے کی بہت کوشش کی۔
of effort much did persuade her by animals All

bekar kuch sab lekin kya bhi majboor us ne Unhon
انہوں نے اسے مجبور بھی کیا لیکن سب کچھ بیکار۔
useless thing all but did also compelled her by Them
in vain everything tried to force They

hota shuroo bajay barah vaqt ka khane khana ke Sher
شیر کے کھانا کھانے کا وقت بارہ بجے شروع ہوتا
would start time twelve time of to eat meal of tiger (The)
hour

tin aur ghayi ho der kafi to aur is lekin tha
تھا لیکن اس روز تو کافی دیر ہو گئی اور تین
three and went is time quite a lot of then day this but was

ghaye baj
بج گئے۔
went time
hour

kar shuroo chelaana ne xargosh hi achanek kar Aakhir
آخر کار اچانک ہی خرگوش نے چلانا شروع کر
do start to run by hare (the) just suddenly action Finally

ghar Aur ghaya bach Main ghaya bach Main bola aur diya
دیا اور بولا "میں بچ گیا میں بچ گیا۔" اور غار
cave And went off I went off I spoke and gave

ghaya ho ravana tar ki
کی طرف روانہ ہو گیا۔
went is depart direction to

sher bhuka ke dekha ne us to ghaya qarib vuh Jab
جب وہ قریب گیا تو اس نے دیکھا کہ بھوکا شیر
tiger hungry that saw by him then went close she When

tariqa xuzubnak aur hai raha chir ko zamin men khusa
غصہ میں زمین کو چیر رہا ہے اور غضبناک طریقہ
manner angry and is being rip to earth in anger

hai raha dahar se
سے دہاڑ رہا ہے۔
is being roar of
in

yih hai kon bola aur cheelaya se khussa Sher
شیر غصہ سے چلاّیا اور بولا "کون ہے یہ
this is Who said and screamed from anger tiger (The)

karaya intizar itna mujhe ne jis xargosh nafirman
نافرمان خرگوش جس نے مجھے اتنا انتظار کرایا۔"
did to wait so me by which hare disobedient
kept waiting

thi majboori Meri diya javab ne Xargosh
خرگوش نے جواب دیا "میری مجبوری تھی"
was compulsion My gave answer by hare (The)
I had to

ho kya majboori Tumhari poocha se is ne Sher
شیر نے اس سے پوچھا "تمہاری مجبوری کیا ہو
is what compulsion your asked from him by tiger (The)

hai sakti
سکتی ہے؟"
is could

number mera aj ke diya javab us ne Xargosh
خرگوش نے اسے جواب دیا کہ آج میرا نمبر
number me to today that gave answer him by hare (The)
turn answered

jo	tha	ka	bhayi	mere	number	to	Aj	tha	nahin
جو	تھا	کا	بھائی	میرے	نمبر	تو	آج	تھا۔	نہیں
who	was	of	brother	my	number the turn	then	Today	was (it)	not

ke	us	to	Main	tha	mota	ziyadah	kahin	se	mujh
کے	اس	تو	میں	تھا۔	موٹا	زیادہ	کہیں	سے	مجھ
to	him	to	in	was	fat	more	a little	from	me

bhayi	Mera	hun	pattla	dubbla	bahut	men	muqablah
بھائی	میرا	ہوں۔	پتلا	دبلا	بہت	میں	مقابلہ
brother	My	am	thin	lean	very	in	comparison

tha	hua	ravane	liye	ke	ghar	ke	ap	par	vaqt	sahih
تھا	ہوا	روانہ	لئے	کے	غار	کے	آپ	پر	وقت	صحیح
was	happened	depart	for	of	cave	of	you	on	time	correct

jo	ghaya	mil	sher	dusra	ek	us	men	raste	lekin
جو	گیا	مل	شیر	دوسرا	ایک	اسے	میں	راستے	لیکن
who	went	met	tiger	second	a	him	in	road (the)	but

tha	liya	hi	pakkar	us	ne	Us	tha	chaahta	khana	us
تھا	لیا	ہی	پکڑ	اسے	نے	اس	تھا۔	چاہتا	کھانا	اسے
was	take	just	capture	he	by	Him	was	wanting	eat	him

main	vaqt	ussi	theek	tha	jarha	le	liye	ke	khane	aur
میں	وقت	اسی	ٹھیک	تھا۔	جارہا	لے	لئے	کے	کھانے	اور
I	time	that	Well Just	was	going	take	for	of	food	and

ap	mulk	yih	ke	kaha	se	us	aur	ghaya	pahanch	vahan
آپ	ملک	یہ	کہ	کہا	سے	اس	اور	گیا	پہنچ	وہاں
you	land	this	that	said	to	this	and	went	arrive	there

ko ap jo hai ka sher dusre to yih hai nahin ka
کا نہیں ہے یہ تو دوسرے شیر کا ہے جو آپ کو
to you who is of tiger other (an) then this is not of

is par Is gha de sazza ki haarkut is
اس حرکت کی سزا دے گا۔ اس پر اس
this on This will give punishment to misdemeanour this

balla ko sher is aur Jao diya javab ne sher ajanabi
اجنبی شیر نے جواب دیا "جاؤ اور اس شیر کو بلا
call to tiger this and Go gave answer by tiger strange

gha karun larayi sath ke is main phir aur lao
لاؤ اور پھر میں اس کے ساتھ لڑائی کروں گا۔"
will do fight with to him I then and bring

kar le pegham ka ussi to main Janaab
جناب میں تو اسی کا پیغام لے کر
do take message to that then I Sir
taking

ko sher makaar is ap taakki hun aya pas ke ap
آپ کے پاس آیا ہوں تاکہ آپ اس مکار شیر کو
to tiger false this you so that am came by to you
to you went

sikhay sabaq usse kar maar
مار کر اسے سبق سکھایں۔
teach lesson him do kill

nafrat aya khusa bahut kar sun bat yih ko Sher
شیر کو یہ بات سن کر بہت غصہ آیا نفرت
hate came anger much do hear thing this to tiger (The)

us aur ghaya ho pagel vuh men alam ke ghamand aur
اور گھمنڈ کے عالم میں وہ پاگل ہو گیا اور اس
him and went is crazy he in condition to pride and

sher vuh dekhen aur chalen Ao kaha se xargosh ne
نے خرگوش سے کہا "آؤ چلیں اور دیکھیں وہ شیر
tiger this see and let's Go said to hare (the) by
Let's go

marne ko sher dushmen hi donon vuh Aur hai kaunsa
کونسا ہے۔" اور وہ دونوں ہی دشمن شیر کو مارنے
kill to tiger enemy just both they And is which

parey chel liye ke
کے لئے چل پڑے۔
lay move for of
left

xargosh to the rahe barh agay log vuh Jab
جب وہ لوگ آگے بڑھ رہے تھے تو خرگوش
hare (the) then were being increase forward people these When
moved along

ke tha raha lug aissa tha raha log hua dhera kafi
کافی ڈرا ہوا لگ رہا تھا ایسا لگ رہا تھا کہ
that was being look such was being look is fear quite
as if he looked afraid looked

hai diya chupa picche ke chari kisi ko xud ne us
اس نے خود کو کسی جھاڑی کے پیچھے چھپا دیا ہے۔
is gave hide back of bush some to self by him
would hide

dere itna hua kya Ab poocha se is ne Sher
شیر نے اس سے پوچھا "اب کیا ہوا، اتنا ڈرے
fear so much is what Now asked from him by tiger (The)

ho kyon hue
ہوئے کیوں ہو؟"
is why was

hun raha der liye is Main diya javab ne Xargosh
خرگوش نے جواب دیا "میں اس لئے ڈر رہا ہوں
am being fear for this I gave answer by hare (The)

aa qarib bahut hamare ghar ka sher dusre kyonki
کیونکہ دوسرے شیر کا غار ہمارے بہت قریب آ
come close very us cave of tiger other (the) because

hai ghaya
گیا ہے۔"
is went

adjib men aankhoon ki sher kar sun bat ki Is
اس کی بات سن کر شیر کی آنکھوں میں عجیب
weird (a) in eyes of tiger (the) do hear thing to This
hearing

ko sher dusre ne us aur ghayi ho peda chamak si
سی چمک پیدا ہو گئی اور اس نے دوسرے شیر کو
to tiger other (the) by him and went is born shine of

se xargosh aur diya kar shuroo karna talash udhar idhar
ادھر ادھر تلاش کرنا شروع کر دیا اور خرگوش سے
from hare (the) and gave do start to do search here here
everywhere

hai kahan batao Mujhe bola
بولا "مجھے بتاؤ کہاں ہے۔"
is where tell Me spoke

hai Vahan diya javab ne Xargosh
خرگوش نے جواب دیا "وہاں ہے
is There gave answer by hare (The)

pas ke paidon ke ap
آپ کے پیروں کے پاس۔"
by to feet of you
by your feet

de nahin dekhayi ghar koyi to Muhje bola Sher
شیر بولا "مجھے تو کوئی غار دکھائی نہیں دے
give not see cave any then Me spoke tiger (The)

ghar mujhe kar bhar agay hi xud Tum hai raha
رہا ہے۔ تم خود ہی آگے بڑھ کر مجھے غار
cave me do increase forward just self You is being
moved along

dekhate nahin kyon
کیوں نہیں دکھاتے؟"
show not why

mujhe ap pahle lekin Zaroor diya javab ne Xargosh
خرگوش نے جواب دیا "ضرور لیکن پہلے آپ مجھے
me you first but Sure gave answer by hare (The)

uthalin men hath apne
اپنے ہاتھ میں اٹھالیں۔"
take in hand your

men hath apne ko xargosh chaalaak ne sher liye Is
اس لئے شیر نے چالاک خرگوش کو اپنے ہاتھ میں
in hand his to hare cunning (the) by tiger for This

chalne par raste hue bataye ke is aur liya utha
اٹھا لیا اور اس کے بتائے ہوئے راستے پر چلنے
to walk on ways (the) be tell of this and take take

kinare ke koyen ghare ek sher bad der Kuch laga
لگا۔ کچھ دیر بعد شیر ایک گہرے کوئیں کے کنارے
edge of well deep a tiger (the) after while Some apply

ghaya pahanch par
پر پہنچ گیا۔
went arrive on

kan ke sher ne Xargosh ghar ka sher is hai Yih
"یہ ہے اس شیر کا غار۔" خرگوش نے شیر کے کان
ear to tiger (the) by hare (The) cave of tiger this is This

vuh dekhiye andar bola aur kaha se chupke men
میں چپکے سے کہا اور بولا اندر دیکھیے وہ
there look inside spoke and said from surreptitiously in
said quietly

ga jaye dekh hi ap apne ko ap
آپ کو اپنے آپ ہی دکھ جائے گا۔
will go see just you his to you

jhanka andar ne us jab hokar khare par Kinare
کنارے پر کھڑے ہوکر جب اس نے اندر جھانکا
peep inside by him when be do standing up on edge (The)
peer being

ka xargosh aur apna men tali ki koyen us to
تو اسے کوئیں کی تلی میں اپنا اور خرگوش کا
of hare (the) and his own in bottom of well (the) him then

شیر
tiger

dushman apna ne us jissey diya dekhayi aks
عکس دکھائی دیا جسے اس نے اپنا دشمن
enemy his by him whom gave saw reflection

اور
and

samjha bhaji ka is ko aks ke xargosh
خرگوش کے عکس کو اس کا بھائی سمجھا۔
understood brother of him to reflection of hare (the)

taraf ek ko xargosh phurtiley aur chaalaak ne Us
اس نے چالاک اور پھرتیلے خرگوش کو ایک طرف
direction one to hare quick and cunning (the) by Him

nichay hi sath ke dahaar zordar ek xud kar de dakaa
دھکا دے کر خود ایک زوردار دہاڑ کے ساتھ ہی نیچے
under just with of roar strong one self do give push

di laga challangk
چھلانگ لگا دی۔
gave apply jump

paon hath apne tak der kafi andar ke Pani
پانی کے اندر کافی دیر تک اپنے ہاتھ پاؤں
foot hand his up to while enough inside of water (The)

Aur ghaya ho xamoosh liye ke hamisha vuh bad ke marnee
مارنے کے بعد وہ ہمیشہ کے لئے خاموش ہو گیا۔ اور
And went is quiet for of always he after of strike
dead

se mydad ki xargosh ko jaanvaron ke jangal like is
اس طرح جنگل کے جانوروں کو خرگوش کی مدد سے
from help to hare (the) to animals of forest like this

se hukumaran zalim ek
ایک ظالم حکمراں سے
from ruling tyrant one

ghayi mil nijat liye ke mesha
میشہ کے لئے نجات مل گئی۔
went meet salvation for of skin
saved their skin

ولی داد اورجنت کی پریاں
Wali Dad and the Fairies of Paradise

ولی داد اور جنت کی پریاں
Peris of Paradise (the) and Dad Wali
Fairies

شہر سے دور مٹی کی ایک جھونپڑی میں ولی داد
Dad Wali in hut one of mud far off from city (The)
in a mud hut

نام کا ایک گھاس کاٹنے والا شخص رہتا تھا۔
was staying person one cutting grass one of name
grass-cutter

ہر صبح ولی داد جنگل سے ڈھیر ساری گھاس کاٹ کر
do cut grass all heap from forest Dad Wali morning Every

اسے گٹھری سے باندھتا اور دوپہر کو بازار
marketplace to afternoon and bind would from bundle him

لے جا کر اسے خریداروں کو چارے کے طور پر
on as to fodder of buyers him do go take
as

بیچ دیا کرتا تھا۔
was doing gave sell
sold

اس کی کمائی ہر روز تین پیسہ ہوتی تھی
was being paisa (monetary unit) three day every earnings of This

جس میں تیس سکے ہوتے تھے۔ دس سکے کھانے
food coins ten .were would have been were coins thirty in which

میں خرچ ہوتے تھے۔ دس سکے کپڑے اور دوسری ضرورتوں
needs second other and clothes coins Ten .were be expense in

میں خرچ ہوتے تھے اور باقی کے دس
ten of remaining and were would have been were expense in

سکوں کو وہ ایک مٹی کے برتن میں بچاکر رکھتا تھا۔ وہ اس
this He .was kept save in pot of clay one he of coins

برتن کو اپنے بستر میں نیچے رکھتا تھا۔
was kept under in bed his to pot

اس طرح ولی داد کافی سالوں تک سکون کی
to easily up to years enough Dad Wali like This

زندگی گزارتا رہا۔
remained passing through life lived

ایک شام ولی داد نے اپنے سارے پیسوں کو گننے کے
of counting of money all his by Dad Wali evening One

لئے اس برتن کو باہر نکالا۔ وہ یہ دیکھ کر کافی خوش
happy enough do see this He pulled out out to pot this for

ہوا کہ مٹی کا برتن پیسوں سے پورا بھر گیا ہے۔
is went total full from money pot of clay that was

اس نے خود سے سوال کیا "اس پیسہ سے میں کیا
what in from money This did question from self by Him

کروں گا میرے پاس تو وہ سب کچھ ہے جس کی مجھے
me to which is some all this then by me will do

ضرورت ہے؟"
is need

ولی داد کافی دیر تک اسی بات کو سوچتا رہا
being thought of matter that about while enough Dad Wali

اور آخیر میں اس کے دماغ میں ایک خیال آیا۔
came idea one in brain of this one in last and

اگلے دن ولی داد نے سارے پیسوں کو ایک تھیلے میں
in bag one to money all by Dad Wali day next (The)

بھرا اور اسے بازار میں ایک سنار کے پاس لے
take by of goldsmith one in market (the) he and filled

گیا۔ اس نے اس پیسہ سے سونے کا ایک خوبصورت سا
of beautiful one of gold from money this by Him went

دست بند خریدا۔
purchased band hand
bracelet

ولی داد وہاں سے ایک سوداگر کے پاس گیا جو دنیا
world who went by of merchant one from there Dad Wali

بھر کا سفر کر چکا تھا۔ ولی داد نے اس سے پوچھا۔
ask from him by Dad Wali was done do travel of whole

"کیا تم مجھے یہ بتا سکتے ہو کہ دنیا میں سب سے
from all in world what is can tell this me you What

زیادہ شریف عورت کون سی ہے؟"
is of who woman noble more

سوداگر نے اسے جواب دیا "یہاں سے مشرق کی
merchant (The) by him answer gave here from east of

طرف ایک ملک ہے جس کا نام خائستان ہے۔ اس
direction one country is which of name Khaistan is This

ملک کی ملکہ سب سے زیادہ شریف اور نوجوان ہے
country of queen all from more noble and young is

کیونکہ میں اکثر اس کے محل میں جاتا ہوں۔ وہاں
because I often her of palace in would go am There

جانے میں تین دن کا سفر طے کرنا پڑتا ہے۔"
go in three day of travel fixed to do have to is

ولی داد نے اس سے کہا "میرے ساتھ ایک مہربانی کریں۔
Wali Dad by him from said Me with for one kindness do

اگلی بار جب آپ اس راستے سے گزریں تو یہ چھوٹا
Next time when you this road from pass then this small

سہ دست بند میری مبارک باد کے ساتھ ان کو
of hand band bracelet my congratulations blessing speech of with her to

پیش کر دیں۔"
give do offer

سوداگر اس پھٹے حال گاس کاٹنے والے کو
to master cutting grass condition ragged this merchant (The)

دیکھ کر حیران تھا کہ ماجرہ کیا ہے لیکن وہ اس بات
thing this he but is what affair that was surprise do see

پر راضی ہو گیا کہ وہ دست بند کو ملکہ تک
up to queen (the) to band hand he that went is willing on
the bracelet

پہنچا دے گا۔
will give arrived

جب سوداگر خائستان کی ملکہ کے دربار میں پہنچا
arrived in palace of queen of Khaistan merchant (the) When

تو اس نے وہ دست بند ولی داد کی طرف سے اسے
to her from side to Dad Wali band hand that by him then
bracelet

تحفہ میں پیش کیا۔
did offer in gift

ملکہ کو وہ دست بند کافی پسند آیا اور اس نے
by her and came like quite band hand that to queen (The)
liked bracelet

اس کی کافی تعریف کی۔ اس نے سوداگر سے کہا کہ
that said from merchant by Her did praise enough to him

ہماری طرف سے اپنے دوست کو ہمارا تحفہ پیش کر دینا
to give do offer gift our to friend your from side our

اور اپنے نوکروں کو حکم دیا کہ ایک اونٹ پر بہترین
best on camel one that gave order to servants her and

ریشم لاد دیا جائے۔
go gave load silk

جب سوداگر واپس آیا تو ریشم کو ولی داد کی
to Dad Wali to silk then came back merchant (the) When

جھونپڑی پر لے کر پہنچا۔
reached do take on hut

اس تحفہ کو دیکھ کر ولی داد کے مونھ سے بے ساختہ
made -non from mouth to Dad Wali do see to gift This
untidiness {مُنھ} seeing

نکلا "اوہ نہیں! یہ تو پہلے سے بھی زیادہ برا ہے۔ میں
uttered Oh no This then first from also more bad is I

ان بہتریں کپڑوں کا کیا کروں گا؟"
this fine clothes of what do will

سوداگر نے کہا "بہتر تو یہ ہے کہ تم اسے
(The) merchant by said Better then this is that you it

کسی اور کو دے دو۔"
someone also to give give

ولی داد نے ایک لمحہ کے لئے سوچا پھر وہ
Wali Dad by one moment of for thought then he

سوداگر سے بولا "دنیا میں سب سے زیادہ شریف
(the) merchant from to spoke World in all from more noble

آدمی کون ہے؟"
man who is

سوداگر نے جواب دیا یہ تو بہت آسان ہے اور
(The) merchant by answer gave this then very easy is and

بولا "نیک آباد کا نوجوان شہنشاہ سب سے زیادہ
more from all emperor young of settlement Virtuous spoke
Nekabad (city of)

شریف ہے۔ میں اس کے محل بھی کئی بار جا چکا ہوں
am done go time many also palace of him I is noble

جو تین دن کی مسافحت کے بعد مغرب کی طرف
direction to west after of transportation to day three which

واقع ہے۔"
is situated

ولی داد نے اس سے درخواست کی اور کہا "جب آپ اگلی
next you When said also to offer from him by Dad Wali

بار وہاں جائیں تو یہ ریشمی لباس میری طرف سے
from side my clothing silk this then go there time
from me

ان کو میری مبارک باد کے ساتھ پیش کر دیں۔"
give do offer with of speech congratulations my to him
blessing

سوداگر اس بار بھی حیران ہوا لیکن وہ ایسا کرنے
do such he but was surprised also time this merchant (The)

کے لئے راضی ہو گیا۔ جب وہ اگلی بار
time next he When .went is willing for of

نیک آباد گیا تو شہنشاہ کو وہ سارا ریشم
silk all he to emperor (the) then went settlement virtuous
Nekabad (city of)

تحفہ کے طور پر ولی داد کی طرف سے پیش کیا۔
did offer from side to Dad Wali on as of gift

ریشم کو دیکھ کر شہنشاہ بہت خوش ہوا اور اس نے
by him and was happy very emperor do see to silk (The)

اس کی بہت تعریف کی۔ اس نے سوداگر سے کہا کہ
that said from merchant by Him did praise very to this

میری طرف سے اپنے دوست کو بارہ بہترین گھوڑوں کا تحفہ
gift of horses best twelve to friend your from side my

پیش کرو جو میرے سب سے خاص گھوڑوں میں سے ہیں۔
are from in horses special from all my which do offer

اس بار سوداگر ولی داد کے لئے بادشاہ کے بارہ
twelve of king for of Dad Wali merchant (the) time This

گھوڑوں کا تحفہ لے کر آیا۔
came do take gift of horses

اسے دیکھ کر ولی داد بولا "یہ تو برا ہی ہو رہا ہے۔
.is being is just bad then This spoke Dad Wali do see Him seeing

اب میں ان بارہ گھوڑوں کا کیا کروں؟"
do what of horses twelve those I Now

کچھ دیر کے بعد ولی داد نے کہا "میں جانتا ہوں ان
that am know I said by Dad Wali after of while Some

تحفہ کا اصل حقدار کون ہے۔" اس نے سوداگر سے
from merchant (the) by Him is who entitled really of gift

درخواست کی کہ دو گھوڑے وہ اپنے لئے رکھ لے اور
and take keep for yourself these horses two that to petition

باقی کے گھوڑوں کو وہ خائستان کی ملکہ کے پاس لے
take by of queen of Khaistan this to horses of remaining

جائے۔
go

سوداگر کو بھی کافی مزہ آرہا تھا کیونکہ اس
him because was coming fun enough also to merchant (The)

کو یہ بات کافی عجیب لگ رہی تھی۔ پھر بھی وہ
he also Then was being look weird enough thing this to

راضی ہو گیا۔ جب وہ اگلی بار ملکہ کے محل گیا
went palace of queen time next he When went is willing

تو ان گھوڑوں کو ولی داد کی طرف سے تحفہ کے طور
as of gift from side to Dad Wali to horses these then

پر پیش کیا۔
did offer on

اس بار ملکہ اور بھی حیران ہوئی اور اس نے
by her and was surprise(d) also and queen (the) time This
even more

وزیر اعظم سے اس بارے میں بات کی جو
who did saying in about this to greatest minister
spoke of this prime minister

اس کے پاس ہی بیٹھے ہوئے تھے۔ ملکہ نے اس کے
of him by queen (The) were be sit down just by of her
was sitting next to her

کان میں کہا "ولی داد کیوں اتنے تحفے بھیج رہا ہے، میں
ear in said Dad Wali why so many gifts send being is I

نے تو اس کے بارے میں آج تک سنا بھی نہیں۔"
by then him of about in today up to heard also not

وزیر اعظم نے یہ رائے دی کہ آپ اسے
(The) minister greatest by this counsel is that you him
The prime minister

اس طرح تحفہ بھیجیں کہ دوبارہ اس کی ہمت نہ ہو کہ وہ
this like gift send that again him to dare not is that he
a similar

آپ کو کوئی تحفہ بھیج سکے۔ اسے ایسا تحفہ بھیجا جائے
you to what gift send could Him such gift sent go

جس کے بارے میں اس نے کبھی سوچا بھی نہ ہو اور
which of about in him by ever thought also not is and

جس کی برابری کوئی دوسرا تحفہ نہ کر سکے۔
which to equality what other gift not do could

اس لئے ولی داد کے دس بہترین گھوڑوں کے بدلے میں
This for Wali Dad of ten best horses of change in
in exchange

ملکہ نے اس بار اسے چاندی سے لدے ہو دس خچر
mules ten is load from silver him time this by queen (the)

بھیجے۔
send

جب سوداگر خچروں کے ساتھ اس کی جھونپڑی پر
on hut to him with of mules (the) merchant (the) When

لوٹا تو ولی داد انہیں دیکھ کر اور بھی زیادہ رنجیدہ
sad more also and do see them Dad Wali then returned

ہوا اور روتے ہوئے بولا میں نے ایسا کچھ بھی نہیں کیا
did not also some such by I spoke be crying and was
me became

جو اتنا بڑا تحفہ مجھے دیا جائے۔ اس نے سوداگر
merchant by Him go gave to me gift great (a) such which

سے کہا "دوست، ایک بوڑھے آدمی پر رحم کرو، دو خچر
mules two do mercy on man old one Friend said from

تم رکھ لو اور باقی کے خچروں کو نیک آباد کے
of settled pious to mules of remaining and lay keep you
Nekabad

شہنشاہ کے پاس لے جاؤ۔"
go take by of emperor

یہ سن کر سوداگر بہت زیادہ بے چین ہوا لیکن پھر
then but was calm not much very merchant do hear This
anxious hearing

بھی وہ اس بہترین تحفہ کا انکار نہیں کر سکا۔ تھوڑے
little (A) .could do not refusal of gift excellent him he also

عرصہ بعد ہی وہ شہنشاہ کے محل پہنچ گیا اور
and went arrive palace of emperor (the) he just after while

چاندی سے لدے ہو خچر اسے ولی داد کی طرف سے پیش
offer from side to Dad Wali him mules is load from silver

کیے۔
did

بادشاہ بھی اس عجیب سے تحفہ کو دیکھ کر حیران
surprise(d) do see to gift from strange this also king (The)

ہوا اور اس نے بھی اپنے وزیر اعظم سے
from greatest minister his also by him and was
prime minister

صلاح مشورہ کیا۔
did advice counsel
mutual consultation

اس نے رائے دی کہ "ولی داد یہ چاہتا ہے کہ وہ
he that is wanting this Dad Wali that gave counsel by Him

اپنے آپ کو آپ سے بہتر ثابت کر سکے۔ کیوں نہ
not Why can do proven better from you to you himself

اسے ایسا تحفہ بھیجا جائے جس کے آگے ہر تحفہ
gift every in front to which go sent gift such him

حقیر اور ناقص ہو۔"
is poor and lowly
surpasses

اس لئے شہنشاہ نے اسے اس بار ایک عظیم الشان تحفہ
gift divine great one time this him by emperor (the) for This

بھیجا جس میں سونے کی پازیب والے بارہ اونٹ، سونے
gold camel(s) twelve ones anklet(s) to gold in which sent

کی لگام اور رکاب والے بیس گھوڑے، بیس ہاتھی
elephant(s) twenty horse(s) twenty ones stirrup and bridle of

جن کی پیٹھ کو سونے کی کرسیوں سے سجایا گیا تھا
was went decorated from chairs of gold on back of which
saddles

اور ان سبھی جانوروں کی دیکھ بھال کرنے کے لئے بیس
twenty for of do good see to animals all them and
take care

وردی پوش نوکر شامل تھے۔
were included servant posh livery

جب سوداگر نوکر اور جانوروں کو لے کر
do take to animals and servant(s) (the) merchant (the) When
taking

ولی داد کی جھونپڑی پر پہنچا تو وہ بیچارہ گھاس
grass poor that then arrived on hut of Dad Wali

کاٹنے والا وہاں پاس ہی کھڑا تھا۔ اس دیکھ کر وہ
he do see This .was standing just by there one cutting
seeing

بولا "کیا میری بدنصیبی کبھی ختم نہیں ہوگی۔ برائے
For will be not finish ever misfortune my What spoke

مہربانی ایک لمحہ کے لئے بھی یہاں نہ ٹھہریں۔ ہر جانور
animals All wait not here also for of moment one kindness

سے دو اپنے لئے رکھیں اور باقی کو
to remaining (the) and put it take yourself two from

خائستان کی ملکہ کے لئے لے جائیں۔"
go take for of queen of Khaistan (the)

اس بار سوداگر ناراض ہو کر بولا کہ وہ
he that spoke do is angry merchant (the) time This

بار بار کسی کے پاس کیسے جا سکتا ہے؟ لیکن ولی داد
Dad Wali But is can go how by of some time time
again and again

نے اس سے زور دیکر وہاں جانے کے لئے کہا اور
and told for of to go there give-do force from him by
stressed

کافی درخواست کی تو وہ صرف ایک بار اور وہاں جانے
go there also time one only he then to petition enough

کے لئے راضی ہو گیا۔
went is willing for of

اس بار تو ملکہ ولی داد کے تحفہ کو دیکھ کر یہ
this do see to gift of Dad Wali queen (the) then time This

سوچ نے پر مجبور ہو گئی کہ آخر وہ چاہتا کیا
what wanting he finally that went is compelled on by thinking

ہے کیونکہ اسے ایسے شاندار تحفہ کی کوئی امید نہیں تھی۔
was not hope what to gift beautiful such him because is

ملکہ نے دوبارہ وزیر اعظم سے پوچھا تو اس
him then asked from greatest minister again by queen (The)
the prime minister

نے جواب دیا "لگتا ہے وہ آپ سے شادی کرنا چاہتا
wanting to do wedding from you he is Looks gave answer by
It looks like

ہے۔ اس کے تحفہ بہترین ہیں آپ کو اس سے ملنا چاہیے۔"
should to meet from him to you are best gift of This is

اس لئے ملکہ نے ایک بہت بڑے کارواں کو تیار کرنے
do ready to caravan large very one by queen (the) for This

کا حکم دیا جس میں ان گنت گھوڑے، اونٹ اور
and camel(s) horses countless that in which gave order of

ہاتھی شامل تھے۔ اس سفر کے لئے سوداگر
merchant (the) for of journey This were involved in elephant(s)

کو خاص طور پر اس کارواں میں شامل کیا گیا

went did involved in in caravan this on as selected to

تاکہ وہ راستہ بتا سکے لیکن سوداگر کی حالت کافی

enough state to merchant but can tell way to he so that

خراب تھی کیونکہ ایک انجانے خوف کی وجہ سے وہ

he from reason to fear knowledge one because was bad

کانپ رہا تھا۔

was being trembling

کئی دنوں تک چلنے کے بعد قافلہ نے ایک جگہ اپنا

his place one by the convoy after of to walk up to days Many
for

پڑاؤ ڈالا۔ ملکہ نے سوداگر کو ولی داد کے پاس

by to Dad Wali to merchant (the) by queen (The) threw stop
stopped

بھیجا اور کہاں کہ اسے ہمارے آنے کی اطلاع

notification (a) of to come our he that said and sent
arrival

دو۔

give

جب ولی داد کو ملکہ کے آنے کی خبر ہوئی تو
then was news to to come of queen to Dad Wali When

اس نے اپنا سر پکڑ لیا اور گھبرا گیا اور روتے ہوئے
was crying and went panic and take grasp head his by him

سوداگر سے بولا کہ اب اسے اپنی تمام بیوقوفیوں کی
to fooleries all his him now that said by merchant (the)
to

سزا ضرور ملے گی۔ میری اپنی احمقانہ حرکت
misdemeanour silly my Me will meet sure punishment

کی وجہ سے میری، تمہاری اور ملکہ کی بے عزتی
respect -non to queen and your mine from reason to

ہوئی۔ ہم کیا کریں؟
do what We were

سوداگر نے بڑے سکون کے ساتھ جواب دیا کہ اب
now that gave answer with of peace great by merchant (The)
calm

کچھ بھی نہیں ہو سکتا اور یہ کہہ کر وہ واپس
back he do say this and can is not also something
saying he can do

قافلہ کی طرف لوٹ گیا۔
went return direction to the convoy

اگلی صبح ولی داد صبح سویرے اٹھا اور اپنی
his and take early morning Dad Wali morning next (The)
got up

جھونپڑی سے بولا "الوداع، میری پیاری پرانی جھونپڑی۔ اب
Now hut old sweet my bye bye spoke from hut
to

شاید تم سے دوبارہ کبھی مالاقات نہ ہوگی۔"
will be not meet ever again from you probably

بوڑھا ولی داد سڑک کی طرف چل پڑا لیکن وہ
he but laid move direction to road (the) Dad Wali old (The)

کچھ قدم ہی چلا ہو گا کہ پیچھے سے اسے کسی نے
by some him from back that will is move just step some

آواز دی "ولی داد، تم کہاں جا رہے ہو؟"
is being go where you Dad Wali is voice

جیسے ہی ولی داد پیچھے مڑا اس نے دیکھا کہ دو
two that look by him turned back Dad Wali just Like
turned around As

خوبصورت عورتیں اس کے سامنے کھڑی ہیں جن کے چہرے

face of who are standing in front of him women beautiful

گلاب کی طرح نازک اور روشنی کی طرح چمک رہے ہیں۔ وہ

He are being shine like of light and fragile like of rose

ایک ہی بار میں سمجھ گیا کہ یہ تو جنت کی

to heaven then this that went understand in time just one

کوئی پریاں ہیں۔

are fairies some

پریوں کو دیکھ کر ولی داد اپنے گھٹنوں کے بل بیٹھ کر

do sit bent of knees his Dad Wali do see to fairies (The)

sank on

رونے لگا اور چلّایا "میں ایک بے وقوف بوڑھا آدمی ہوں

am man old sense -non a I exclaimed and apply cry

foolish cried

مجھے اپنے راستے جانے دو۔ میں اپنی رسوائی اور

and disgraceful my I give go road my to me

.let (you)

شرم سار حرکتوں کا سامنا نہیں کر سکتا۔"

can do not confront of antics head shame

shameful

ایک پری نے جواب دیا "ایسے انسان کی رسوائی
disgrace to human being such gave answer by fairy One

تو ہو ہی نہیں سکتی۔ اگر تمہارے کپڑے پھٹے ہوئے ہیں
are being ragged clothes your If can not just is then

تو کیا ہوا تم دل سے تو راجا ہو۔" اور یہ کہکر
saying this And is raja king then from heart you was what then

اس پری نے اس کے کندھے کو چھوا جس کے ساتھ ہی
just with of which touch to shoulder of him by fairy this

ولی داد کے پھٹے ہوئے کپڑے بہترین لباس میں تبدیل
change in clothing fine clothes being ragged of Dad Wali

ہو گئے۔ ہیروں اور جواہرات سے جڑی ہوئی ایک پگڑی
turban {puggaree} one were inlaid from jewelry and Diamonds went is

اس کے سر پر دکھائی دینے لگی۔ اس کی کمر سے
from waist to Him apply give see on head of him

بندھی ہوئی زنگ آلودہ درانتی اب ایک شاندار چمکتی
shining beautiful a now sickle sullied covered rust happened tied up

ہوئی تلوار بن گئی تھی۔
was gone make sword being

اب دوسری پری نے اس سے کہا "ولی داد واپس
back Dad Wali said from him by fairy second (the) Now

لوٹ جاؤ۔ ہر چیز ایسی ہے جیسی ہونی چاہیے۔"
should be like is such thing every go return

ولی داد نے اپنے پیچھے مڑ کر دیکھا اور یہ دیکھ کر
do see this and look do turn back his by Dad Wali

حیران ہو گیا کہ اس کی پرانی جھونپڑی غائب ہو گئی
gone is missing hut old to him that went is surprise

تھی اور اس کی جگہ ایک شاندار محل دکھائی دے رہا
being give see palace beautiful one place of its this and was

تھا جو سورج کی روشنی میں جگمگا رہا تھا۔ گھبراکر
In a panic was being shine in light to the sun which was

وہ پریوں کی طرف مڑا لیکن وہ
they but turned direction to fairies (the) he

غائب ہو چکی تھیں۔
were finished is missing
had already vanished

ولی داد تیزی سے واپس سڑک کے کنارے کنارے چلنے لگا۔
apply to walk edge edge of road back from fast Dad Wali

جب وہ محل میں داخل ہوا تو دربانوں نے
by concierge (the) then was enter in palace (the) he When

اسے سلام کیا اور نوکر اس کے سامنے جھک کر
do bow in front of him servant(s) (the) and did greeting him

ادب سے کھڑے ہو گئے۔ کچھ نوکر مہمانوں کی
to guests servant(s) Some went is standing from reverence
waiting

استقبال کی تیاریوں میں مصروف ہو گئے اور
and went is busy in preparations to welcome

ادھر ادھر دوڑنے لگے۔
started to run here here
here and there

ولی داد محل کے انگنت کمروں میں گھومنے لگا۔
started to roam in rooms infinite of palace (the) Dad Wali

اپنی امیری کو دیکھ کر اس کا منہ کھلا کا کھلا ہی رہ
stay just open of open mouth of him do see to wealth His
wide open

گیا۔ اسے یقین ہی نہیں ہو رہا تھا کہ وہ کسی
some he that was being is not just belief To him went

شاندار محل میں گھوم رہا ہے۔ وہ اپنے خیالوں میں گم
lost in thoughts his He is being roam in palace beautiful

تھا کہ تبھی تین نوکر دوڑتے ہوئے آئے اور
and came was running servant(s) three then that was
when

ان میں ایک نے کہا "مشرق کی طرف سے ایک بڑا سا
of great one from direction of east said by one in them
on of them

قافلہ آ رہا ہے۔" دوسرے نے اس کی بات کاٹی
severed word to this by other (The) is being come convoy
interrupted

اور کہا "قافلہ مغرب کی طرف سے آ رہا ہے۔"
is being come from direction to west convoy (a) said and

تبھی تیسرے نے ان دونوں کی بات کاٹی اور کہا
said and severed word to both of them in by third Then
interrupted

کہ دو قافلے دونوں سمتوں سے آ رہے
being come from directions both of them caravans two that

ہیں۔
are

پریشان ہوکر ولی داد باہر کی طرف آیا جہاں دو
two where came direction to out Dad Wali passing Upset

قافلے اس کے محل کے سامنے آکر رکے تھے۔ مشرق
East were stop will in front of palace of him caravan(s)

سے ملکہ اپنے تخت پر سوار ہو کر آئی تھی جس
which was came do is riding on throne litter her queen (the) from

میں ہیرے جواہرات جڑے ہوئے تھے اور مغرب سے
from east and were be studded jewelry diamonds in

شہنشاہ اپنے شاندار گھوڑے پر سوار ہو کر آیا تھا۔
was came do is riding on horse beautiful his emperor

ولی داد جلدی سے ملکہ کی طرف دوڑا۔
ran direction to queen from haste Dad Wali

خائستان کی رانی نے اس سے کہا "میرے پیارے ولی داد،
Dad Wali dear my said from him by queen to Khaistan

آخر ہم مل ہی گئے!" جب ملکہ کی نگاہ شہنشاہ پر
on emperor sight to queen When went just meet we Finally

پڑی تو اس نے پوچھا کہ یہ بہرتین شہنشاہ کون
who emperor magnificent this that asked by her then had to

ہے؟
is

ولی داد نے جواب دیا "عالی جاہ، یہ
this ok Excellent gave answer by Dad Wali

نیک آباد کے شہنشاہ ہیں۔" اور اس سے اجازت
permission from him And is emperor of settlement virtuous
Nekabad (the city of)

لینے کے بعد وہ شہنشاہ کی طرف دوڑا۔
ran direction to emperor he after of to take

نیک آباد کے شہنشاہ نے ولی داد کو دیکھ کر کہا
said do see to Dad Wali by emperor of settlement Virtuous
Nekabad (The)

"میں اس انسان سے ملنا چاہتا تھا جو مجھے
me who was wanting to meet from person this I

شاندار تحفے بھیجتا ہے۔" لیکن جب اس کی نظر ملکہ
queen sight to him when But is would send gifts beautiful

پر پڑی تو اس نے ولی داد سے اس کے بارے میں
in about of him from Dad Wali by him then had to on

پوچھا۔
asked

اور جب دونوں نے ایک دوسرے کو دیکھا تو انہیں
them then look to other (the) one by both of them when And

ایک دوسرے سے محبت ہو گئی اور کچھ ہی دنوں کے
of days just some and gone is love from other (the) one

بعد ان دونوں کی شادی ولی داد کے محل میں
in palace of Dad Wali wedding to both of them they after

ہو گئی۔ شادی کی تقریب کئی دنوں
days many ceremony to wedding gone is

تک چلتی رہی۔
stayed running up to
lasted

اس تقریب کے بعد شہنشاہ اپنی ملکہ کو لے کر
do take -to- queen his emperor (the) after of ceremony This
taking

نیک آباد چلا گیا اور ولی داد اپنے محل میں
in palace his Dad Wali and went move Settlement Virtuous
to Nekabad

اکیلا رہ گیا۔
went stay alone

اگلی صبح ولی داد بہت جلدی اپنے بستر سے اٹھا
take from bed his hastily very Dad Wali morning next (The)

اور بہت ہی خاموشی کے ساتھ محل سے نکلنے کے
of exit from palace (the) with of silence just very and

بعد سڑک کی طرف چلنے لگا۔
apply to walk direction to road after
started

لیکن وہ کچھ ہی قدم چلا ہوگا کہ پیچھے سے ایک
one from back that will be moved step(s) just some he But
as

آواز نے اسے روک لیا۔ "ولی داد، تم کہاں جا رہے ہو؟"
are being go where you Dad Wali took stop him by voice
stopped

اس نے دیکھا کہ وہی پریاں اس کے پیچھے کھڑی ہیں
are standing behind of him fairy same that look by Him

جنھوں نے اس کی زندگی کو بدل دیا تھا۔ وہ دوبارہ اپنے
his again He was gave change to life to him by who

گھٹنوں پر گر گیا اور رونے لگا۔ پریوں کے سامنے
in front of fairy apply cry and went fall on knees

گڑگڑاتے ہوئے اس نے ان سے کہا "میں نے آپ سے
from you by I said from in by him be gurgledimplored
Me

کہا تھا کہ میں ایک بوڑھا بیوقوف آدمی ہوں۔ جو کچھ
some who am man foolish old one I that was said

مجھے ملا ہے میں اس کا بہت شکر گزار ہوتا لیکن
but would be paying thankful very of this I is found to me

"----------

....

دوسری پری نے کہا "ولی داد، کچھ مت کہو۔ تہمارے
(The) second fairy by said Wali Dad anything don't say Your

دل کی مراد ضرور پوری ہوگی۔"
heart of intent sure wholly will be
heart's desire fulfilled

اور یہ کہکر اس نے اسے دوبارہ چھوا۔
and this saying her by him again touched

اس طرح ولی داد اپنی پرانی زندگی میں دوبارہ لوٹ آیا
This like Wali Dad his old life in again return came

جس میں وہ گھاس کاٹ کر اور اسے بیچ کر بہت خوش
which in he grass cut do and him between do very happy

تھا۔ اس نے اپنی زندگی دوبارہ سے شروع کی اور اپنی
was Him by his life again from start did and his
old life started

باقی کی زندگی بہت خوشی اور سکون سے گزاری۔
remaining of life very happy and easy from time

حالانکہ وہ اپنے دوست شہنشاہ اور ملکہ کو
Although he his friend(s) emperor (the) and queen (the) to

بہت یاد کرتا تھا لیکن اس نے انہیں دوبارہ کوئی
very remember doing was but however him by them again what

تحفہ بھیجنے کی غلطی نہیں کی۔
gift to send to mistake not made

شہزادہ بیرم اور پریوں کی دلہن
Prince Bairam and the Fairy Bride

شہزادہ بیرم اور پریوں کی دلہن
Bride of Fairies (the) and Bairam Prince
the Fairy Bride

ایک بار کی بات ہے کوہ کاف کی پہاڑیوں میں
in mountains to Kaf Koh is thing to time One
in the mountains of Koh Kaf Once upon a time there was

بہت سارے دیو رہا کرتے تھے جو کافی طاقتور تھے۔
were powerful quite who were do being giant(s) all very
lived lots of

ایک بار ان کے راجا نے انسانوں کی دنیا
world to humans by king -of- their time One
the human world

میں جانے کا ارادا کیا۔ اس راجا کا نام صیفید تھا۔
was Safeyd name of king This did intention of go in
wanted to visit

زمین پر آنے کے بعد وہ ادھر ادھر گھومنے لگا اور
and applied to roam there here he after of to come on Earth
roamed around after arriving on earth

گھومتے گھومتے ایک جنگل میں پہنچ گیا۔ اس نے دیکھا
saw by Him went arrive in forest one walking walking
arrived walking a long time

کہ جنگل میں شکاریوں کی ایک ٹولی ایک ہرن کا
of deer a group one to hunters in forest that
a group of hunters

پیچھا کر رہی ہے۔ شکاریوں کی یہ ٹولی
group this of hunters is being do chase
The group of hunters were chasing

جنگل میں مزہ کرنے اور شکار سے لطف اندوز ہونے
to be enjoy enjoyment from hunt and do fun in forest
merry by the hunt had fun in the forest

کے لئے آئی تھی۔ ان کا سردار ایک نوجوان شہزادہ تھا
was prince young a chief of Them was came for of
Their became

جس کا نام بیرم تھا۔ وہ نوجوان اتنا خوبصورت تھا
was beautiful so youth That was Bairam name of which
whose

کہ اسے دیکھتے ہی صیفید کو ایسا لگا کہ اسے اس
him him to that felt such to Safeyd just see him that

سے کوئی لگاؤ ہو گیا ہے کیونکہ اس کی خوبصورتی
beauty to him because is went is attachment some from

میں ایک الگ سی کشش تھی۔ اسے ایسا لگا کہ
that appeared such Him was attraction of distinct a in

اگر یہ شہزادہ اسے مل جائے تو خوشی ہر وقت
time every happiness then go meet him prince this if
be with

اس کے پاس رہے گی لیکن اگر شہزادہ اسے نہیں ملا تو
then met not him prince if but will being by of him
be with

پھر وہ خوشی کے لئے ہمیشہ ترستا رہے گا۔
will being crave always for of happiness he then

اس لئے صیفید نے خود کو ایک شاندار گھوڑے میں
in horse beautiful one to self by Safeyd for This
into a horse

تبدیل کر لیا جس کی کھال برف کی
to snow skin (the) of which took do change
a snow blanket of which changed

چادر کی طرف سفید تھی اور ہنہناہٹ بجلی
bolt (a thunder) neigh (the) and was white side to sheet
as a snow blanket

کی گرج کی طرف سخت۔ اپنی اس شکل میں اس نے
by him in shape him His hard side to thunder of
as

شہزادے کا راستہ کئی بار کاٹا تاکہ اس کا
of him so that cut time(s) many path of prince (the)
crossed

دھیان اپنی طرف کھینچ سکے۔
could pull direction his heed
attention

اتنے شاندار گھوڑے کو دیکھ کر شہزادہ اتنا مسحور
enchanted so prince (the) do see to horse beautiful (a) Such

ہو گیا کہ اس نے حکم دیا کہ اس گھوڑے کو پکڑ
capture to horse him that gave order by him that went is

کر لاؤ۔ صیفید کو اس بات سے کافی خوشی ہوئی اور
and was happy quite from thing this to Safeyd bring do

یہی وہ چاہتا تھا کہ اس پر زین کسی جائے اور
and go some saddle on him that was wanted he like that

لگام ڈالی جائے۔ صیفید شہزادے سے اس قدر مسرور
delighted prize this from prince (the) Safeyd go gave bridle

ہو گیا کہ وہ چاہتا تھا کہ وہ اس کی پیٹھ پر
on back (the) to him he that was wanting he that went is

چھلانگ لگائے۔ جیسے ہی اسے لگا کہ شہزادہ حفاظت
safe prince (the) that apply him just Like applied jump
Just as jumped

کے ساتھ اس کی پیٹھ پر بیٹھ گیا ہے اس نے سرپٹ بھاگنا
fled gallop by him is went sit on back to him with of

شروع کر دیا۔ وہ راستے میں بھی کہیں نہیں رکا اور اسی
that and stop not a little also in road He gave do start
did not stop at all on the road

وقت اپنی رفتار دھیمی کی جب وہ اپنے محل میں ان
these in palace his he when to slow speed his time
until

پہاڑیوں سے داخل ہوا جنہوں نے زمین کو چاروں
all four to earth by which was enter from mountains

طرف سے گھیر رکھا تھا۔ وہاں اس نے شہزادہ
prince (the) by him There was kept surround from direction(s)

کا پورا خیال رکھا اور زندگی کو آرام دینے والی
being give comfort to life and placed regard whole of
giving completely took care

ہر چیز مہیا کی۔ اس پر سونے اور قیمتی جواہرات
jewelry valuable and gold on Him did provided thing every

کی بارش کردی۔ اس کے لئے شاندار گھوڑوں اور
and horses beautiful for of Him made rain to

نوکر چاکر کا انتظام کیا۔ اسے بہترین اور قیمتی
valuable and fine Him did disposition of servant(s) servant(s)
domestic servants

لباس پہننے کو دیے اور اسے ایک شاندار محل میں
in palace beautiful one him and gave to to wear clothing

قیام کرایا۔
did-come stay

آٹھ دنوں کے بعد وہ دیو بیرم کے پاس آیا اور اس
him and came by of Bairam giant that after of days Eight

سے کہا کہ میں اٹھ دنوں کے لئے اپنے بھائی کی
to brother his for of days eight in that said from

شادی میں جا رہا ہوں لیکن تم یہیں رہو گے۔ اس
This would stay here you but am being go I wedding

دیو نے اسے ایک چابی دی تاکہ وہ اندر والے باغ
garden being inside he so that gave key one him by giant
inner (the)

میں داخل ہو سکے۔ اس دیو نے اسے بتایا کہ اس باغ
garden this that told him by giant This could is enter in

میں اس کے سوا کوئی بھی داخل نہیں ہو سکتا کیونکہ
because can is not enter also anyone except to him in

یہ باغ صرف صیفید کا ہے۔ اس نے اسے تاکید کی
to emphasis this by Him is of Safeyd only garden this

کہ جب وہ باغ میں جائے تو اکیلا جائے واپس
back goes alone then goes in garden (the) he when that

آنے پر دروازے کو تالا لگانا بالکل نہ بھولے۔
forget (it) not much applies lock to doors (the) on to come

اس لئے دیو نے شہزادہ کو چابی دی اور
and gave key (that) to prince (the) by giant (the) for This

فورا اپنے بھائی کی شادی کے لئے روانا ہو گیا۔
went is sped for of wedding to brother his immediately

بیرم اسی شام باغ میں داخل ہوا۔ باغ
garden (The) was enter in garden (the) evening that Bairam

میں داخل ہونے کے بعد اس کی حیرت کی انتہا نہ
not extremely to surprise to him after of to be enter in

رہی کیونکہ اس نے آج تک اتنا خوبصورت باغ

garden beautiful (a) such up to today by him because being

پہلے کبھی نہیں دیکھا تھا۔ باغ اتنا خوبصورت تھا کہ

that was beautiful so garden (The) was look not ever first

اس کا تصور بھی نہیں کیا جا سکتا۔ تالاب کے

of pond (The) could go did not also imagination to him

could imagine (it) he

نیچے کا حصہ سنگ مردار سے بنا تھا جسے قیمتی

valuable which was make from marble stone part of bottom

was made marble

پتھروں سے جڑا گیا تھا۔ فوارے چاروں طرف

direction(s) all four fountains (The) was went inset from stones

چل رہے تھے۔ پھلوں کے بجائے پیڑوں پر بیش قیمتی

valuable sure on trees instead of Fruits were being move

یاقوت، زمرد اور نیلم لدے ہوئے تھے۔ وہ کچھ

some He were be load sapphire(s) and emerald(s) ruby

were loaded rubies

دیر کے لئے نیچے بیٹھا اور ان فواروں سے

from fountains those and sit down under for to while

with sat during

لطف اندوز ہونے لگا جن سے سنہری رنگ کی تیز
fast to color golden from which felt be enjoy pleasure
enjoyed

پانی کی دھار نکل رہی تھی اور جس کا عکس
reflection of which and was being get out spout of water

خوبصورت تالاب میں بھی دکھائی دے رہا تھا۔
was being give see also in pond beautiful

ٹھیک اسی وقت چار فاختہ جن کا رنگ دودھ کی
to milk (of) color (the) of which dove(s) four time that Right
of which

طرح سفید تھا، ایک پیڑ کے اوپر سے اڑتی ہوئی آئیں اور
and come on was flew from top of tree one was white like
came flying

چار خوبصورت پریوں میں تبدیل ہو گئیں اور ایک تالاب کے
of pond one and go is change in fairies beautiful four

کنارے بیٹھ گئیں۔ اس تالاب کا پانی اتنا صاف شفاف
transparent clear so water (the) of pond This go sit edge

تھا کہ تالاب کے اندر کی ہر چیز صاف دکھائی
see clear thing every to inside of pond (the) that was

دے رہی تھی۔ ان کی خوبصورتی سے شہزادہ کی

to prince (the) from beauty to This was being give

آنکھیں چندیا گئیں۔چندیا گئیں۔

went dazzle eyes

were dazzled

انہوں نے اپنے کپڑے اتارے اور نہانے لگیں۔ جب

When started to bathe and taken off clothes their by Them

وہ نہا رہی تھیں تو ان میں سے ایک نے کہا "میں

I said by one from in them then were being bathe they

My by one of them were bathing

نے ایک خواب دیکھا جس کے مطابق ہم میں سے

from in us in accordance of which see vision one by

from us

کوئی ایک باقی لوگوں سے الگ ہو جائے گی۔"

will go is separate from people remaining one some

will be the others

نہانے کے بعد ان میں سے ہر ایک باری باری اپنے

their turn turn one every from in they after of bath (The)

کپڑے پہنے کے لئے تالاب سے نکلنے لگی لیکن ان میں

in them but apply exit from pond for of wear clothes

سب سے خوبصورت پری کے کپڑے غائب تھے۔ دوسری

other (The) were missing clothes of fairy beautiful from all
the most

پریوں نے اپنے کپڑے تبدیل کیے اور اپنی پہلی شکل میں

in shape first their and did change clothes their by fairies

لوٹنے کے بعد اڑ کر چلی گئیں۔ یہ چوتھی پری جس

which fairy fourth This went go do flew after of to return

کا نام گلاب بانو تھا چلا کر اپنی ساتھوں کو خدا

good -to- friends her do cry was Bano Ghulab name of
cried Rose Queen

حافظ کہتی رہی اور بولی "یہ میرا نصیب ہے۔ میری دوسری

other my is fate me to this said and being says bye
said

قسمت یہاں میرا انتظار کر رہی ہے اور ایسا لگتا ہے

is appears such and is being do awaiting me to here destiny

کہ ہم دوبارہ کبھی نہیں ملیں گے۔"

would meet not ever again we that

پھر اس نے تالاب کے کنارے کی طرف دیکھا اور

and look direction to edge of pond (the) by her Then
she

شہزادہ کو دیکھ کر حیران رہ گئی۔
went remain surprise(d) do see to prince (the)
was seeing

اسے لگا کہ اس کا دل اس کے جسم سے باہر
out from body of her heart of her to affection Him
her body her heart Out of love for him

آ گیا ہے کیونکہ اس نے کسی انسان کے یہاں
here of human being some by her because is went come
went

ہونے کی امید نہیں کی تھی۔ شہزادہ کو دیکھ کر
do see to prince (The) was of not expectation to to be

اسے اس سے محبت ہو گئی۔
went is love from her to him

پری کو یہ بات معلوم نہیں تھی کہ شہزادہ نے
by prince (the) that was not know thing this to fairy (The)

ہی اس کے کپڑے چھپائے تھے۔ لیکن اس نے ایسا اس لئے
for him such by him But were hide clothes of her just

کیا تھا تاکہ وہ دوبارہ ان کپڑوں کو پہن کر فاختہ
dove do wear to clothes these again he so that was what

نہ بن جائے اور وہ اس سے ہمیشہ کے لئے محروم ہو
is deprived for of always from him he and go make not

جائے۔ وہ اس کے لئے دوسرے کپڑے لایا جنہیں پہننے
to wear which brought clothes other for to her He go

کے بعد پری بہت زیادہ خوبصورت لگ رہی تھی۔
was being look beautiful much very fairy (the) after of

اس طرح پری شہزادہ کے ساتھ ہی رہنے لگی اور
and started stay just with of prince (the) fairy (the) like This

انہیں اس بات کا احساس ہی نہیں ہوا کہ آٹھ دن
day(s) eight that was not just feeling of thing this them
not noticed it they

گزر گئے ہیں۔ شادی ختم ہونے کے بعد صیفید
Safeyd after of to be finished wedding (The) are went pass
passed

اپنے گھر واپس لوٹ آیا۔ لیکن اچانک بیرم نے خود کو
to self by Bairam suddenly But came return back home his

ایک چین میں گھرے ہوئے محسوس کیا جو اس کی
of him which did felt was surrounded in chain one

کمر کے ارد گرد بنی ہوئی تھی۔ اسے دیکھ کر
do see This was were done around wrapped of waist
seeing

بیرم ڈر سے کانپنے لگا۔ لیکن دیو نے اسے
him by giant (the) But apply to tremble from fear Bairam
started to tremble

یقین دلایا کہ وہ محفوظ ہے اور اس سے کہا "ڈرتے
Scared said from him and is safe he that convinced believe

کیوں ہو! تمہارے پاس بھی وہی ہے جو میرے پاس ہے۔"
is by my which is same (the) also by You is why
of mine Yours

دیو نے حکم دیا کہ موسیقی شروع کی جائے اور
and go to start music that gave order by giant (The)

رقاصاؤں سے کہا کہ وہ اسے خوش کرنے کے لئے اس کے
of him for of do happy him he that said from dancers

سامنے بہترین ناچ پیش کریں، لیکن عجیب بات یہ تھی
was this thing weird but do offer dance best in front

کہ وہاں کچھ بھی دکھائی نہیں دے رہا تھا۔
was being give not see also some there that
anything

پھر دیو نے خود ہی اس سے پوچھا "کیا تمہیں کچھ
some you What asked from him just self by giant (the) Then

دکھائی دے رہا ہے؟"
is being give see

شہزادہ نے جواب دیا کہ اسے دکھائی تو کچھ
some then see him that gave answer by prince (The)
anything

بھی نہیں دے رہا ہے لیکن موسیقی کی رسیلی آواز اور
and voice juicy to music (the) but is being give not also

پائلوں کی کھنکھناہٹ اسے صاف سنائی دے رہی ہے۔
is being give listen clear him ringing to anklets

تب دیو نے اس سے کہا "میں تمہیں حضرت سلیمان
Solomon Saint to you I said from him by giant (the) Then
King

کا سرمہ دونگا جسے لگانے کے بعد تم ہر اس
this every you after of to apply which will give antimony of

چیز کو دیکھ سکتے ہو جو دکھائی نہیں دے رہی ہے۔"
is being give not see which is could see to thing
is invisible

دیو نے اس سے کہا کہ اپنی آنکھوں پر یہ
this on eyes his that said from him by giant (The)

سرمہ لگاؤ۔
apply antimony

جب شہزادہ نے اپنی آنکھوں میں حضرت سلیمان کا
of Solomon Saint King in eyes his by prince (the) When

سرمہ لگایا تو وہ یہ دیکھ کر حیران رہ گیا کہ
that went stay surprise do see this he then applied antimony

محل پر کشش اور خوبصورت نوجوان لڑکیوں کی ٹولیوں
groups to girls young beautiful and attractive on palace

سے بھرا ہوا ہے جو سارنگی اور تبلے کی دھن پر
on tune to drums and sarangi {Indian violin} who is was full from

ناچ رہی ہیں۔
are being dance

اسے حیرانی اس بات کی ہوئی کہ جس پری کو اس نے
by him to fairy that that was of thing this surprise Him

روکا تھا وہ دیو کی رانیوں میں سے ایک تھی

was one from in queens to giant (the) that was stopped

from the giant's

اور دیو کو اس بات کی پوری خبر تھی جو اس

him who was known wholly to thing this to giant (the) and

کے پیچھے محل میں ہوا تھا۔ لیکن بیرم سے اسے

to him from Bairam But was being in palace twists of

adventures

اس قدر محبت ہوئی کہ اس نے اس سے کہا "اگر

If said from him by him that was love (of) price (the) this

تم چاہو تو گلاب بانو کو لے سکتے ہو اور اس کے

of him and is could take to Bano Ghulab then want you

Rose Queen

ساتھ ہی میری ہر چیز پر تمہارا اختیار ہوگا جو

which will be authority your on thing every my just with

possession

میرے پاس ہے۔"

is by my

of me

ایک دن پری بہت اداس ہو گئی اور اس نے بیرم

Bairam by him and went is upset very fairy (the) day One

سے کہا کہ اسے اپنے ماں باپ سے ملنے جانا ہے
is go to meet from father mother his him that said from

اور ان سے ملنے کے بعد وہ واپس آ جائے گی۔
will go come back she after of to meet from them and

یہ سن کر بیرم اس کے پری والے کپڑے لے آیا۔ اس
Her came take clothes type fairy of him Bairam do hear This
brought the fairy clothes hearing

نے وہ کپڑے پہنیں اور فاختہ بننے کے بعد اسے
her after of to become dove (a) and put on clothes these by

الوداع کہکر وہاں سے اڑ گئی۔ جب پری کے والدین
parents of fairy When went flew from there saying bye(good)
flew away

کو یہ بات معلوم ہوئی کہ اس نے کسی انسان سے
from human being some by her that was know thing this to

شادی کی ہے تو وہ بہت غصہ ہوئے۔ پری کو
to fairy (The) was anger much they then is to wedding
as they were very angry

سزا دینے کے لئے انہیں نے اسے ایک ایسے اندھیرے شہر
city dark such one her by them for of give punishment

میں قید کر دیا جو زمین کے اندر تھا۔
was inside of earth who gave do lock up in

جب کافی وقت گزر گیا اور پری نہیں لوٹی
returned not fairy (the) and went pass time enough When
had passed

تو شہزادہ بیرم کافی اداس ہو گیا اور مایوسی اور غم
grief and despair and went is upset quite Bairam prince then
became

کی وجہ سے گھلنے لگا۔ اسے دیکھکر دیو
giant (the) by looking Him seemed pine away from reason to
Seeing him so

کی حالت بھی خراب ہو گئی اور وہ بھی اداس اور افسردہ
sorry and upset also he and went is bad also state -to-
became

ہو گیا۔
went is

جب انتظار کی انتہا ہو گئی تو وہ چلّایا "میں
I exclaimed he then went is finished to to await When

اسے تلاش کرنے جا رہا ہوں اور اس وقت تک
up to time this and am being go do search her
until this time will

نہیں لوٹوں گا جب تک اسے تلاش نہ کر لوں۔"
will take do not find her up to when will return not
I will find her until will not return

دیو نے اس سے پوچھا "کیا تم نے واقعی میں ایسا
such -in- really by you What asked from him by giant (The)
you So

مضبوط ارادہ کر لیا ہے کہ تم اسے ڈھونڈ کر
do search her you that is took do intent strong
search have

ہی لاؤ گے؟" بیرم نے اسے جواب دیا کہ
that gave answer him by Bairam will bring just
will

اپنی بیوی کے بغیر وہ ایک پل بھی
also second one he without of wife his
without his wife

زندہ نہیں رہ سکتا۔
could stay not live
not could live

تب دیو نے اسے تین چیزیں دیں: اپنی ٹوپی جسے
which hat His gave things three him by giant (the) Then

پہننے کے بعد انسان غائب ہوجاتا ہے۔ حضرت سلیمان
Solomon Saint is became hidden person (a) after of to wear
King would become invisible

کا سرمہ اور اپنا ایک بال۔ انہیں لے کر شہزادہ

prince (the) do take Them hair one his and antimony of

taking one of his hairs

پری کی تلاش میں روانا ہو گیا اور کئی دنوں کی

of days many and went is depart in search to fairy (the)

departed in search of the fairy

تلاش کے بعد اس شہر میں پہنچ گیا جو

which went arrive in city (the) him after of search

arrived

زمین کے اندر تھا لیکن اسے وہاں کچھ دکھائی نہیں

not see anything there him but was inside of earth (the)

دے رہا تھا کیوں وہ شہر پورا اندھیرے میں ڈوبا

drowning in dark wholly city that because was being give

could

ہوا تھا۔ تب اس نے اپنی آنکھوں میں سرمہ لگایا

applied antimony in eyes his by him Then was was

جسے لگانے کے بعد ہر چیز آئینہ کی طرح صاف

clear like to mirror thing every after of to apply which

ہو گئی اور ہر چیز دکھائی دینے لگی۔

apply give see thing every and went is

became visible became

جب اس نے شہر میں چھان بین شروع کی
of start looking investigation in city (the) by him When
to investigate

تو اسے معلوم ہوا کہ گلاب بانوں کو ایک بہت ہی
very much one to Bano Ghulab that was known him then
Rose Queen

اونچے قلعہ میں قید کیا گیا ہے جس میں
in which is went did imprisonment in castle high
in which was tower

لوہے کے سو دروازہ ہیں۔ جب وہ قلعہ کے سامنے
in front of fort (the) he When are door(s) hundred of iron
hundred iron

آیا تو اپنی ٹوپی کو اپنے سر پر لگایا جسے
which put on head his to hat his then came

لگاتے ہی وہ غائب ہو گیا۔
went is hidden he just putting
became invisible when putting on

ٹوپی کو لگاتے کے ساتھ ہی لوہے کے سارے دروازے بھی
also doors all of iron just with of apply to hat (The)
all the doors of iron By putting on the hat

پوری طرح کھل گئے۔ شہزادہ قلعہ میں داخل ہوا اور
and was enter in fort (the) prince (The) went open like whole
entered opened wide

جب اسے شہزادی پری دکھائی دی تو اس نے اپنی
his by him then is see fairy princess (the) to him when
he saw the fairy princess he

ٹوپی اتار لی اور اس کے گلے لگ گیا۔ وہ وہاں اس
her there He went apply neck of him and apply take off hat
embraced took off

کے ساتھ کئی دنوں تک رہا۔
remained up to days many with of

لیکن افسوس کوئی بھی عورت کسی راز کو
to secret any woman also what woe But
a secret whoever

زیادہ دنوں تک چھپاکر نہیں رکھ سکتی اور گلاب بانوں
Bano Ghulab and can keep not hiding up to days more
Rose Queen could more than a few days

نے بھی بہت جلد اس راز کو اپنی کچھ خاص نوکرانیوں
servants certain some her to secret this soon very also by

کو بتا دیا۔ اس نے یہ بات اپنی کچھ خاص سہیلیوں کو
to friends certain some her thing this by her gave tell to

بھی بتائی کہ اس کی اچھے دنوں کی شروعات ہو گئی
went is getting started of days good of this that tell also

ہے اور بہت جدل اسے اس قید سے آزادی
freedom from confinement this to her separation much and is

ملنے والی ہے۔ اس طرح یہ خبر اس کے باپ تک جا
go up to father of her news this like This is like to meet
way

پہنچی اور اس نے اپنے تمام دیووں کو جمع کیا اور
and did collect to giants all his by him and arrived

قلعہ کی طرف روانہ ہو گیا۔ وہاں پہنچ کر اس نے
by him do arrive there went is depart direction to fort (the)

دیکھا کہ شہزادہ شہزادی کے ساتھ رہ رہا ہے۔
is being stay with of princess prince that see

انہیں دیکھ کر وہ بہت زیادہ غضب ناک ہو گئے اور
and went is inflamed anger more very he do see Them

چلا کر بولے "اسے جان سے مار دو!"
give kill from life To him spoke do cry
Take his life crying out

شور سن کر شہزادے کی آنکھ کھل گئی جو پاس
by who went open eye to prince (the) do hear noise (The)

میں سو رہا تھا۔ انہیں دیکھ کر اس نے فورا اپنی
his immediately by him do see Them was being sleep in

ٹوپی پہنی اور غائب ہو گیا۔ پھر اس نے صیفید کا دیا
gave of Safeyd by him Then went is hidden and wore hat
became invisible

ہوا بال نکالا اور اسے چراغ کی آگ کے سامنے کر
do in front of fire to oil lamp to it and pulled out hair was

دیا جس سے وہاں ایک عجیب سا دھواں پھیلنے لگا اور
and apply spread smoke of weird one there from which gave

وہ دھواں دیووں کی ایک بہت بڑی فوج میں تبدیل ہو گیا
went is change in army big very one of giants smoke this

جس میں ایک ہزار مسلح سپاہی تھے۔ دونوں گروپوں میں
in groups Both were soldiers armed thousand one in which

زوردار لڑائی ہونے لگی اور شہزادہ کی فوج کی جیت
win of army of prince (the) and apply to be fight strong

ہوئی۔ پری کے باپ نے اپنی ہار تسلیم کر لی اور
and took do admit defeat his by father of fairy (The) were

اپنی لڑکی کو بیرم کو سونپ دیا۔ اس کے بعد صیفید،
Safeyd after of him gave give up to Bairam to girl his

شہزادہ اور اس کی رانی جیت کے ساتھ اپنے خوبصورت
beautiful their with of win queen to him and prince (the)
in triumph his

محل میں لوٹ آئے۔
came return in palace

اسی طرح کئی سال گزر گئے اور شہزادہ کو اپنی
his to prince (the) and went pass year(s) many like That
passed

دنیا کی یاد ستانے لگی۔ اس کی یاد اتنی
so much memory to Him apply torment memory of world
longing tormented longing

بڑھ گئی کہ اس نے اپنی دنیا میں جانے کا فیصلہ
decision of go in world his by him that went increase

کر لیا۔ دیو کو یہ سن کر بہت مایوسی ہوئی
happened sad very do hear this to giant (The) took do

لیکن وہ شہزادے سے بہت محبت کرتا تھا اس لئے اس
him for him was doing love much from prince (the) he but
loved

نے اسے جانے کی اجازت دے دی۔
is give permission to go him by
gave

گلاب بانو نے خود کو ایک بہت بڑی چڑیا میں
in bird big very one to self by Bano Ghulab
Rose Queen

تبدیل کر لیا اور شہزادے سے کہا کہ وہ اس کے
of her he that said from prince (the) and took do change
changed

دونوں پروں کے بیچ میں بیٹھ جائے۔ کچھ ہی دیر میں
in while just Some go sit in between of wings both

وہ دونوں اپنے ملک کی راجدھانی کے پاس اتر گئے۔
went descent by of capital of country his both they
landed

وہاں شہزادے نے خود کو ایک فقیر کے شکل میں پیش
offer in shape of poor one to self by prince (the) There
disguise

کیا اور اس کی بیوی ایک سفید فاختہ میں بدل گئی۔
went change in dove white one wife to him and what
changed

پھر وہ شہر میں داخل ہوا اور اپنی بوڑھی دائی
midwife old his and was enter in city (the) he Then
nurse entered

سے ملاقات کی جو اسے دیکھکر فورا

immediately by looking him who to meeting from

پہچان گئی۔ اس نے اسے بتایا کہ اس کے وزیر نے

by minister of him that told him by Her went recognize

recognized

حکومت پر قبضہ کر لیا ہے اور اس کے بجائے

instead of him and is take do occupation on government

took over

خود حکومت چلا رہا ہے۔

is being move government self

is running

بیرم نے اس سے پوچھا کہ اس کی بیویاں کہاں ہیں۔

are where wives to him that asked from him by Bairam

اس نے بتایا کہ تمہاری تین بیویوں کو وہ اپنی بیویوں کے

of wives his he to wives three your that told by Her

پاس لے گیا لیکن چوتھی بیوی نے اس کی مخالفت

opposition to him by wife fourth (the) but went take by

کی تو اس نے اسے ایک گڈھے میں قید کر دیا ہے۔

is gave do confinement in pit one him by him then to

imprisoned in a dungeon

وہاں اسے ایک لڑکا ہوا اور دونوں ماں اور بیٹا
son and mother both also was boy one to her There

صحیح سلامت ہیں۔ بوڑھی عورت نے اسے یہ بھی بتایا
told also this him by woman old (The) are security correct
safe and sound

کہ وہ انہیں اپنے شکاری کتوں کا بچا کھچا کھانے کو
to food joints scrap of dogs hunting his them he that
as food leftovers

دیتا ہے جس پر ان کی زندگی چل رہی ہے۔
is being move life to them on which is give
alive kept gives

کچھ مدت کے لئے شہزادہ اپنی دائی کے ساتھ ہی
just with of nurse his prince (the) for of period Some

رہا اور اسی دوران پری نے اپنی اصل شکل
shape real her by fairy (the) during that and stayed

اختیار کر لی۔ لیکن ایک دن جب شہزادہ کسی کام
work some prince (the) when day one But took do adopted
assumed

سے باہر گیا تو یہ خبر اس مکار بادشاہ تک
up to king false (the) him news this then went out from

پہنچ گئی کہ بوڑھی عورت کے مکان میں دنیا کی
to world (the) in house of woman old (an) that went arrive
the world's

سب سے حسین عورت رہتی ہے۔
is lived woman beautiful from all
is living most

اس لئے مکار بادشاہ وہاں آ پہنچا اور اس نے
by him and arrived come there king false (the) for This
visited

گلاب بانو کو پکڑ لیا اور چلا کر اس سے بولا
spoke from this do move and take capture -to- Bano Ghulab
moving her caught Rose Queen

"میرے ساتھ چلو۔"
go with Me

گلاب بانو اپنا ہاتھ چھڑاتے ہوئے اس سے بولی "اوہ
Oh told from him be freed hand her Bano Ghulab
Rose Queen

بادشاہ، پہلے مجھے اندر جاکر اپنے کپڑے بدل لینے دو۔"
give take change clothes my go inside me first king

بادشاہ اس کی بات مان گیا اور دروازے پر
on door (the) and went accept thing (the) to her king (The)
at

اس کا انتظار کرنے لگا۔ جب شہزادی اپنے کمرے میں

in room her princess (the) When apply do await -of- her
awaited

داخل ہوئی تو اس نے اپنا پری کا لباس پہنا جسے

of which wore clothing of fairy her by her then was enter

پہن کر وہ ایک سفید فاختہ میں تبدیل ہو گئی اور

and went is change in dove white one she do wear
changed wearing

کھڑکی کے راستے وہاں سے آزاد ہو گئی۔ اور اس طرح

like him And went is free from there road of window (the)

مکار بادشاہ ہار کا صدمہ لئے وہاں سے غمگین ہو کر

do is sad from there for trauma of defeat king false

اپنے محل واپس لوٹ گیا۔

went return back palace his
returned

جب بیرم واپس لوٹا تو اس نے پہلا سوال

question first (the) by him then returned back Bairam When

یہی کیا کہ اس کی بیوی کہاں ہے۔

is where wife to him that what like that

بوڑھی عورت نے اسے بتایا کہ وہ وزیر کے ساتھ
old (The) woman by him told that that minister of with

جا چکی ہے۔ وزیر اسے اپنے ساتھ زبر دستی
go took is minister (The) her himself with great manual
was taken with force

لے گیا۔
take went

شہزادے نے دوبارہ دیو کا دیا ہوا بال نکالا
prince (The) by again giant (the) of gave was hair pulled out
given

اور اسے آگ کی لپٹ کے سامنے کیا۔ اس کی مدد کے لئے
and him fire to flame of in front did This to help of for

فورا ہی ہزاروں دیو جمع ہو گئے جن
immediately just thousands giant(s) (of) together is went which
came

کے ہاتھوں میں لمبی لمبی تلواریں تھیں۔ انہوں نے پورے
of hands in long long swords were them by entire (the)

شہر پر قبضہ کر لیا۔ وزیر اور اس کی تینوں
city on occupy do took minister (The) and him to all three

مکار بیویوں کو قتل کر دیا گیا۔ اس کی چوتھی وفادار

loyal fourth to Him went gave do murder to wives false

did

بیوی کو قید سے آزاد کرا لیا گیا اور دوبارہ

again and went take do free from confinement to wife

did

سے رانی بنا دیا گیا۔

went gave make queen (the) from (her)

made

اپنی رانی کے ساتھ بیرم کچھ عرصہ تک رہتا رہا اس

him being lived up to time some Bairam with of queen His

نے اسے کسی بات کی کوئی پریشانی نہیں ہونے دی لیکن

but gave to be not problems any to thing some to him by

were

اسے اپنی پریزاد بیوی کی کمی ہمیشہ

always lack of to wife fairy-born his him

کھلتی رہی جو اپنے والدین کے گھر واپس

back home of parents her who remained consumed

'parents pined for

اڑ کر چلی گئی تھی اور دوبارہ کبھی واپس نہیں آئی۔

came not back ever again and was went go do flew

had flown

اس کی اداسی اور غمگینی اس حد تک بڑھ گئی
went increase up to range this grief and sadness to Him
increased so To his grief

کہ وہ اس کی تنہائی میں پاگل ہو گیا وہ شہر، محل
palace city that went is crazy in isolation to him it that
became

اور جنگلوں میں اپنے کھوئے ہوئے پیار کو پاگلوں کی طرح
like to crazy to love being any(where) his in forests and
lost

تلاش کرنے لگا۔
apply do search

اسی بیچ دیو صیفید کا حال بھی
also condition of Safeyd giant (the) between This
Meanwhile

کچھ ایسا ہی ہو گیا۔ وہ بھی شہزادہ کی محبت میں
in love of prince (the) also He went is just such some
became like that

بہت غمگین ہو گیا اور ایک دن اس نے اپنے دوست کی
to friend his by him day one and went is sad very
became

دنیا میں جانے کا فیصلہ کر لیا۔ اس نے اسے
him by Him took do decision of to go in world

تلاش کر لیا اور اپنے ساتھ لے جاکر اسے دوبارہ
find do take and himself with take go him again
found taking

پریوں کی شہزادی کے ساتھ بحال کر دیا۔
fairy (the) of princess of with restore do gave
the fairy princess restored

اپنے کھوئے ہوئے پیار کو واپس پاکر بیرم کی
His any(where) being love to back having found Bairam to
lost

صحت دوبارہ اچھی ہو گئی اور اس کی بعد کی ساری
health again good is went and him to after to all

زندگی خوشیوں اور مسرتوں میں گزری۔ کبھی وہ
life happiness and cheer in passed by Sometimes he

گلاب بانو کے ساتھ کوہ کاف کی پہاڑیوں میں اپنا وقت
Ghulab Bano of with Koh Kaf to mountains in his time

گزارتا تو کبھی اپنی وفادار بیوی کے ساتھ اپنی
spent then sometimes his loyal wife of with his

حکومت کی راجدھانی میں۔
government to capital in

www.ingramcontent.com/pod-product-compliance
Lightning Source LLC
LaVergne TN
LVHW010931110826
845149LV00013B/2549

* 9 7 8 1 9 8 9 6 4 3 2 5 9 *